The Role of the Church in Aging, Volume II

Implications for Practice and Service

The Role of the Church in Aging, Volume II

Implications for Practice and Service

Michael C. Hendrickson, M.Div., M.Th., Ph.D.
Editor

The Haworth Press
New York • London

The Role of the Church in Aging, Volume II: Implications for Practice and Service has also been published as *Journal of Religion & Aging*, Volume 2, Number 3, Spring 1986.

The Haworth Press, Inc., 12 West 32 Street, New York, NY 10001
EUROSPAN/Haworth, 3 Henrietta Street, London WC2E 8LU England

Library of Congress Cataloging in Publication Data

The Role of the church in aging, volume II.

"Has also been published as Journal of religion & aging, volume 2, number 3, Spring 1986"—T.p. verso.
Includes bibliographies.
1. Church work with the aged—Congresses. 2. Aged—Congresses. I. Hendrickson, Michael C.
BV4435.R66   1986   261.8'3426   86-18415
ISBN 0-86656-614-7

The Role of the Church in Aging

Journal of Religion & Aging
Volume 2, Number 3

CONTENTS

The Role of the Church in Aging, Volume II

Implications for Practice and Service

Attaining Ego Integrity Through Life Review

Robert L. Richter, D.Min.

ABSTRACT. This paper is an attempt to provide the theological dimension of Erik Erikson's last stage of life, the crisis of ego integrity versus despair. In this crisis an answer is demanded to the question, "Was my life worthwhile?" A positive or negative verdict must be reached.

The "Life Review" is necessary for the resolution of this conflict. Such a life review is often precipitated by the awareness of death. A few cases are briefly cited to show how elderly patients in a Veterans Administration (V.A.) Hospital setting have coped with this crisis.

Two theological ideas are brought to bear on this problem. One is a review of one's life in connection with James Fowler's idea of "master story," of how effectively we connect with our cherished religious symbols, and the other is Donald Capps's "parabolic event," or how we interpret events in the past as having the potential for new insights.

A new look at repentance and confession is necessary as they are approximate psychological counterparts to these theological teachings.

INTRODUCTION

Erik Erikson's developmental theories have been quoted and interpreted by many behavioral scientists. Daniel Levinson based his book, *The Seasons of a Man's Life* (1978), largely on the work of Erikson. James Fowler applied Erikson's psycho-social development ideas to faith development in his book, *Stages of Faith* (1981).

In his well-known work, *Childhood and Society* (1964), Erikson

Robert L. Richter is Chief, Chaplain Service, William S. Middleton Memorial Veterans Administration Hospital, Madison, Wisconsin. His address is 2500 Overlook Terrace, Madison, Wisconsin 53705.

1

develops the basic theme that from infancy each life stage has a particular crisis which one must weather in order to achieve a happier and more adapted state of existence. For example, the last stage of life revolves around the crisis of ego integrity versus despair. One must reach a verdict based on past experiences whether or not life has been worthwhile. This stage, like the others, is summarized in broad, expansive definition rather than one which is precise and operational.

In his book, *Striking Sails* (1984), Heije Faber, a Dutch clinical pastoral educator, admires Erikson's theories, but feels that his concept of ego integrity versus despair needs further clarification.

> There are, moreover, still other phenomena among the aged which he has not dealt with adequately, such as the preoccupation with the past, the need for an evaluation of their life cycle, and what Erikson includes in the concept of ego integrity: these questions need clarification and a more inclusive theory. (Faber, 1984, p. 107)

LIFE REVIEW IS VITALLY CONNECTED TO EGO INTEGRITY

This paper proposes that the concept of ''life review'' interpreted in a theological way might offer some new perspectives on Faber's questions about the last stage of life.

Life review is a normally occurring reconsideration of the past which focuses on evaluation and may lead to ego integrity or despair.

The concept of life review is more than theoretical. I have listened to the life reviews of many elderly patients in a Veterans Administration Hospital setting. I have noticed that all three elements of Faber's critique of Erikson are present.

An elderly patient looked back on his life as he approached death and concluded, ''I am a failure . . . I always was.'' A ninety-year-old World War I nurse told me the fascinating story of her life and pensively asked, ''Do you think I made any contribution at all?'' Another veteran patient had the deaths of many German soldiers on his mind as cancer weakened him. He confessed that he could not integrate or reconcile this part of his experience with the quiet and caring life he had lived.

The attainment of ego integrity is of critical importance and a negative verdict on one's life is an invitation to despair. The last stage of life is the culmination of all the developmental stages which have preceded, and like all the others, a crisis desperately demanding resolution.

Erikson (1964) uses the word "epigenetic" to describe his developmental theory of crises which occur at various stages. Each stage is influenced by the experience of negotiating, or failing to negotiate, the previous stage. Erikson defines epigenetic, "Everything that grows has a ground plan and out of this ground plan the parts arise, each part having its time and special ascendancy, until all have arisen to form a functioning whole" (Erikson, 1964, p. 34).

Ego integrity is closely connected to the first stage, basic trust. Having trusted life, accepted one's life cycle with no basic regrets, one is able to live with what one has become. The quest for ego integrity finds a person writing the last chapter of life and answering the question, "What has become of me?" with affirmation. The problem of ego integrity is primarily concerned with finding meaning. One finds such meaning in living out the Freudian formula, "lieben und arbeiten" successfully, and "taking care of people and things," to use Erikson's phrase.

The negative side of the crisis of the last stage is despair which leads to self-disgust and self-disdain. Despair is the failure to be affirmed or to affirm life, time, and other people. It is to face death with a sense of dread and failure. It means to give a negative answer to the question posed by life review, "Was it worth it?"

Robert Butler, a well-known psychiatrist concerned with the psychological issues of aging, defines despair as follows:

> Despair expresses the feeling that time is now short, too short for a chance to start another life and to try out alternative roads to integrity. Disgust hides despair if only in the form of a thousand little disgusts which does not add up to one big remorse." (Butler, 1963)

HOW LIFE REVIEW MAY BE PROMPTED

The phenomena of life review often has been written about by those in the helping professions and behavioral sciences. Clements (1984) observes that life review occurs through reminiscences which are necessary in order to face and overcome the blocks and deficits of the past. He proposes ways that such reminiscences may be prompted: engaging in writing; taping an autobiography; experiential genealogy development which considers feelings about significant relationships; scrapbooks and photo albums which recall occasions to talk about; and a summation of one's life work, written or spoken.

Barbara Meyerhoff and Virginia Tofte (1975) feel that life review may be a precipitant of growth and change, an opportunity which accomplishes integration on several levels. In telling their stories the elderly feel a sense of being heard and having their existence over the life span affirmed, thus adding to a more significant sense of being.

THE VERDICT OF LIFE REVIEW—
THE INDIVIDUAL AND SOCIETY

Ego integrity assumes that one is ready to remove oneself from the center of life. In our society this is forced on the elderly and leads to resentment and defensiveness. On the other hand there may be a felt need for withdrawal and a growing inferiority.

Robert Atchley (1972) proposes that the disengagement theory, in which one begins a strategic withdrawal from life in order to deal with closure issues or unfinished business, has an intended function, that society assures its own equilibrium and survival by setting aside those who become less efficient, produce and contribute less. With such usefulness outlived, one gradually withdraws and is replaced.

Institutionalized norms and rites may precede this, but as MacLeish says, characterizing this transition, there are " . . . immobilizing effects of social attitudes which stigmatize the later years as years of decline and fall, of accumulating decay, desuetude, and defeat" (MacLeish, 1976, p. 246).

Life review, arising from withdrawal, human mortality, and the nearness of death, is influenced by the attitudes MacLeish mentions. Society offers its verdict even as an individual is reaching his own verdict about life.

The critical may judge life review as a sign of living in the past, of aimless memories, and pointless escapism, with little sensitivity or regard for its actual purpose and process.

Although for many life review may provide only a nostalgic journey, or mild regrets, some who confront their past are jolted by anxiety, strong feelings of shame and guilt, depression and self-disgust.

Butler (1963) contends that life review plays a significant role in the psychology and psychopathology of the aged. The positive psychological dynamics include a reinterpretation of one's history and a recrafting of one's story in the light of expanded insight. Life review is essential to a reorganization of the personality so that the aged person may achieve wisdom and serenity.

Butler feels that those who tend toward despair possess certain traits or outlooks which dominate their personalities: those so goal-oriented or future-oriented that they merely tolerate the present as it passes them by, and those who have grievously harmed others. The proud and arrogant also will have trouble assimilating the prospect of death.

HOW THEOLOGY RELATES TO LIFE REVIEW AND ATTAINING EGO INTEGRITY

How do these concepts of attaining ego integrity through life review, and the positive or negative verdict about one's life relate to theology? How does theology confront, explore, and grow out of critical developmental and existential issues?

Erikson does not talk theology, but his last stage concept finds Biblical counterparts at many turns, from Moses recounting his leadership efforts on behalf of the people of Israel to Paul's proclamation, "I have fought the good fight . . ."

I find an implicit dialogue going on between Erikson's schema of life stages and Scriptural stories and teachings. For example, the crisis of the young adult, which Erikson identifies as "intimacy versus isolation," connects to the Psalm which reflects upon God as the intimate one. "Jahweh, you examine me and know me, you know if I am standing or sitting, you read my thoughts from far away, whether I walk or lie down, you are watching, you know every detail of my life" (Psalm 139.1-3).

Stage five of Erikson's life stage theory is called "Generativity versus Stagnation," and is a crisis of middle age. This stage's imperative involves taking care of a younger generation by acting as mentor and instructor, and passing down the godly wisdom of tradition. This is a continual theme in the wisdom literature of Scripture. For example,

> And now, my sons, listen to me; listen to instruction and learn how to be wise, do not ignore it. Happy are those who keep my ways! Happy the man who listens to me . . . For the man who finds me finds life, he will win favor from Jahweh. (Prov. 8.32ff.)

THE DEVELOPMENT OF ONE'S MASTER STORY IN THE ATTAINMENT OF EGO INTEGRITY

James Fowler's (1981) idea of stages of faith which parallel Erikson's stages of psycho-social development have been helpful in relating Erikson's last stage of life to theology. Fowler claims, "Erikson has helped us in many ways to focus on the functional aspects of faith, the expected existential issues, which help people cope at whatever structural stage across the life cycle" (Fowler, 1981, p. 109).

Fowler names six stages paralleling Erikson's eight stages of life development. Each of these stages of faith has its own characteristic structure. The first is basic trust, "undifferentiated faith," the foundational stage which follows us over the life span.

Each stage requires efficient ways of expressing faith in how we "grasp, value, evaluate, use symbols and appropriate religious traditions." Through the concept of structural stage we get a new sense "how time, experience, challenge and nurture are required for growth in faith" (Fowler, 1981, p. 115).

We cannot face a new agenda of life phase or crisis with a type of faith structure belonging to a previous stage. If we do, Fowler contends, we will wind up with a narrower and shallower faith than is needed to negotiate the current stage of life.

Fowler also gives us some new insights about the past which expand and explain the concept of life review. The self cannot be obliterated or cancelled. The past needs to be remembered and reworked.

The elderly are not necessarily models of wisdom and serenity. Often their past needs a healing revisitation, revaluing and recomposing. A seventy-nine year-old woman veteran reviewing her life admitted that her mother had never loved her, but favored an alcoholic brother. Her mother had said and done several unkind and uncaring things to her. She had tried to put the past out of mind, but repression was not exactly the royal road to ego integrity. "When you get old you just hope that these things get lost in your memory," she said. Sometimes a painful regression in the service of the ego is needed.

Ann Bedford Ulanov (1983) writes,

> Aging brings home to us what we have done or failed to do with our lives, our creativity or our waste, our openness to zealous hiding from what really matters. Precisely at that point, age cracks us open, sometimes for the first time, makes us more aware of the center, makes us look for it and for relation to it. (Ulanov, 1983, p. 122)

Fowler (1981) also talks about the content of faith which is of critical importance. By content he means what we stake our lives upon, what shapes our perception of life and gives it value, and our master story, the autobiography we are living out derived from core convictions and fundamental principles reflecting the ultimate meaning of our lives.

A master story may be grounded in Scriptural stories which offer new ways to perceive and shape our lives. A master story may emerge in a crisis and provide direction or resolution as it relates to Scriptural counterpart of our own experience. A story is told by one author of a NASA space engineer who was not allowed to finish a project he had conceived and directed. "I felt like Moses unable to enter the Promise land," was the summation of his experience. There is the remembrance of our own prodigality as we face the wayward son in Jesus' parable.

The prophet Nathan's story of the poor man's prized ewe lamb taken by the rich man to feed his guests provided King David with a perspective by which to revisit his past sins and reevaluate his relationship to God. Confession and repentance may be approximate religious counterparts of the psychological dynamic of reinterpreting past events with new insights and understandings. With confession and repentance one may let out and let go of old feelings aroused by shame and guilt and put them to rest. Repentance in the broad sense of the word includes all that God does to bring us to faith, and the attendant response elicited: regret at our irresponsibility, sorrow for hurting others, hope of forgiveness, reparation, reconciliation with God and others, and faith that his Word is true and that God does what he promises.

THE PARABOLIC EVENT AS A WAY OF VIEWING THE PAST

Donald Capps' (1983) key concept of "parabolic event" builds on Fowler's concept of a master story. The master story touches core convictions and encompasses recurring religious themes around which we build our lives. The parabolic event may be a flash of insight gained as our equilibrium is upset and we feel uncomfortable with the stressful and traumatic occurrences of life. The master story unfolds from experience and inner resources. The parabolic event may be a Biblical or environmental cue which serves as a metaphor which provides insight about where God is in the world and where we are in our personal journey.

In an article entitled "Parabolic Events in Augustine's Autobiography" (1983), Capps examines how this famous church dealt with disturbing events of his scandalous past. He faced three significant events which were parabolic in the sense that they pointed to the questions of God's presence in the world and Augustine's concern about what he had become.

The three remembered events were his account of stealing a neighbor's pears, joking about a friend's Baptism, and the vision of a child in a garden who read to him the admonitions against a dissolute life from Romans 13. Facing these events forced him to confront his shameful self and opened him up to the presence of God.

Capps notes the meaning of these parabolic events,

> . . . the self in autobiography is incarnated in concrete events which is another way of saying that the events are parabolic, or metaphorical—they have extensions beyond themselves, they are richly complex images, embodying the secret of a person's life. (Capps, 1983, p. 264)

A parabolic event in the life of a sixty-five year-old patient involved a fatal accident. His report was, "I failed to keep the equipment up," by which he meant he had failed to repair adequately an old car he had purchased. A mechanical failure occurred and his car crashed into another, taking the life of the other driver.

As he examined this event he also discovered an apt metaphor of self and situation. He had failed to "keep the equipment up," by which he also meant his personal failure to keep his health and his relationships smooth and loving because of his alcohol problem.

Yet through the tragic parabolic event of the accident he came to grips with his shame and guilt and was forced to face the utter meaninglessness of his life. His autobiography was bitter, but calamitous enough to gain a clearer picture of what he had become as he looked through the prism of the parabolic. His sense of shame caused deep reflection which helped him face up to foolish, hurtful behavior resulting in regret, dismay, sorrow, and self-disgust.

Through this experience came religious conversion. God's economy of grace extended far beyond this man's shame and self-pitying despair. The integrity of God's grace bestowed on him an alien dignity, despite the harm he had caused.

The expressions of such grace are phrased in the great Biblical metaphors of altar, law court, slave market, and battlefield, those events which were parabolic in the life of Christ as they referred to atonement, acquittal, redemption, and victory.

RELIGIOUS REFLECTION AS AN OLD/NEW WAY OF DEALING WITH THE PAST

The crisis of ego integrity versus despair prompts a new look at dealing with the past, as an objective time frame and as the context of a personal journey. At every predictable crisis of adult life we must deal with the past. Pastoral caregivers need to refocus and reconnect Scripture's stories and insights to the times and seasons of life so that others will see meaning and continuity in life as we go into God's future by God's grace.

A sixty-three year-old farmer dying of leukemia was helped to refocus his past and reconnect himself to vital Biblical stories and teachings which were important in his assertion of ego integrity toward the end of his life. This was done by simply prompting some religious reflection through a few basic questions.

When asked about the function of religion in his life in a personal way he answered,

> Religion means everything to me . . . I think God has been wonderful . . . blessed me with good health all these years until now, and my family has been in good health. Being a farmer

put me in touch with God but I never really knew it . . . seeing all those wonderful things I took for granted.

He marveled over the wonders of creation to which he had been practically oblivious and taken for granted. He further commented on why God had become so meaningful in his illness,

> I'm sometimes amazed at the way he created the world . . . how we get reproduced and are able to love each other except when the devil takes over. Basically we are all good people with exceptions. The universe is too perfect just to happen . . . this is hard to talk about without getting emotionally involved. God gave my parents good health. They died in their eighties. They kept the commandments. I loved them both and always felt I honored them, although sometimes they had their faults, but not many. Mother made sure I was confirmed. Father would never take advantage of another person . . . never heard him swear.

As this patient refocused and reconnected his life to the Biblical story of the creation, he reflected an elemental trust in God, the universe, life processes, and the continuity of relationships. Such affirmation in the face of terminal illness was a grand expression of attaining ego integrity through a life review which personally appropriated the master story of God's creation and providence.

CONCLUSION

The elderly still struggle with what they are and what they ought to be as we all do, and this struggle is not necessarily resolved by the aging process. The church through its pastoral caregivers needs to stand at the threshhold of this difficult crisis of ego integrity versus despair with a listening ear for those who still carry great burdens, fears, and self-accusations.

Pastoral caregivers must learn to recognize life review in progress; how to prompt, coax, and encourage the recrafting of one's story and the reinterpretation of one's history until our master stories merge with the story of him who is "meek and lowly of heart," and our experience of parabolic events help reveal the mystery of the kingdom of God.

REFERENCES

Atchley, Robert. (1972). *The Social Forces in Later Life: An Introduction to Social Geron-tology.* Belmont, CA: Wadsworth Pub. Co.

Butler, Robert. (1963). Life Review: An Interpretation of Reminiscence in the Aged. *Psychi-atry.* 26.

Capps, Donald. (1983). Parabolic Events in Augustine's Autobiography. *Theology Today.* October.

Clements, William. *Care and Counseling of the Aging: Dimensions to Spiritual Develop-ment.* Paper presented at the National Symposium of The Role of the Church and Aging, Zion, Illinois, September, 1984.

Erikson, Erik. (1964). *Childhood and Society.* New York: Norton Pub. Co.

Faber, Heije. (1984). *Striking Sails: A Pastoral View of Growing Older in Our Society.* Nash-ville: Abingdon Press.

Fowler, James. (1981). *Stages of Life.* San Francisco: Harper and Row.

Levinson, Daniel. (1978). *Seasons of a Man's Life.* New York: Knopf Pub. Co.

MacLeish, John. (1976). *The Challenge in Aging: Ullysean Adult Paths to Creative Living.* New York: McGraw-Hill.

Meyerhoff, Barabara & Toft, Virginia. (1975). Life History as Integration. *Gerontologist.* 15(6).

Ulanov, Ann Bedford. (1983). Aging: On the Way to One's End. In William Clements (Ed.), *Ministry with the Aging: Designs—Challenges—Foundations.* San Francisco: Harper and Row.

Pastoral Theological Implications of the Aging Process

Arthur H. Becker, Ph.D.

ABSTRACT. Pastoral care of the aged must deliberately attend to spiritual-theological issues involved in the aging process. As clinical, empirical, and practical pastoral experiences demonstrate, these spiritual-theological problems are as varied as the range of overall problems faced by the elderly. In an attempt to focus on major issues, however, it may be helpful to examine the three epochs of aging i.e., young-old, middle-old, and old-old, in order to determine the spiritual and theological issues which are particularly relevant to each epoch. This paper proposes that each of the three developmental epochs has a main spiritual-theological concern which can be expressed in a question: young-old: "What shall I do with my life?"; middle-old: "What about my dying?"; old-old: "Why must I suffer so?" Pastoral ministry is called to further examine the validity of these assertions and draw practical applications in response to these spiritual-theological issues which face older persons.

Amid the plethora of assessments of aging, the variety of programs advanced for the care of the aged, the significant advances being made in various aspects of gerontology, and the very useful contributions toward understanding the aged coming from the behavioral sciences, there is a danger that the central concern of the church may be overwhelmed or even lost. Pastoral care of the aged too easily may be diverted from its central theme and take on the hues of "counseling" often undifferentiated from that offered by social worker or psychiatrist, or be diverted into various programmatic avenues taking on the hues of recreation therapist or occupational therapist.

The concern for "spiritual well being of the elderly" advanced by the National Interfaith Coalition on Aging (NICA) attempts to

Arthur H. Becker is Norman Menter Professor of Pastoral Theology (Emeritus), Trinity Lutheran Seminary, Columbus, Ohio. His address is 15950 Ringgold Northern Road, Ashville, Ohio 43103.

call us back to our primary task. Antedating, that is, Paul Pruyser's urging that we again assume the responsibilities of genuine pastoral care.[1] He senses a great need for the central message pastoral care of the churches should convey to elders. We need to give more deliberate attention to the spiritual-theological issues involved in the aging process and to the chief task of pastoral persons in the church-pastoral-theological reflection.

It is highly probable that in pastoral ministry with older persons we are guilty of a subtle form of agism that we are not even aware i.e., the tendency to assume that the spiritual or theological problems of those over 65 are out of the same cloth. Studies of aging tell us in no uncertain terms that all old people are not alike. Quite the contrary; they tend to become increasingly unique. Examined pastoral experience, clinical evidence, and what little empirical research has been done in this field suggests that this uniqueness of the elderly is present also in the spiritual domain. It is possibly developmental in character, and very possibly related to the three epochs of aging that have been identified by various scientists.

In this essay, the author suggests that there are specific spiritual-theological issues that are particular to and grow out of the three epochs of aging and that pastoral ministry or care of people has to be sensitive to these developmental specifics. These suggestions are by way of conjectures, or hypotheses, and are offered for empirical, clinical and experiential examination. The author proposes that each of the three developmental epochs, the "young-elderly," the "middle-old" and the "frail-elderly" have spiritual concerns which can be crystallized in a central question. The questions for each of the three phases of aging are:

—For the Young-Old: "What Shall I Do With My life?"
—For the Middle-Old: "What about my dying?"
—For the Frail-Elderly: "Why must I suffer so?"

These questions will only rarely be articulated in the blunt fashion they are put here. But examination of hundreds of student verbatims in ministry with all ages of elderly persons, corroborated by the experience of geriatric chaplains, and finally suggested by the extensive literature dealing with the developmental aspects of aging, have led to these conclusions.

These questions cluster around the four polarities identified years ago by Carl Gustav Jung and more recently revitalized by the studies of Levinson—the polar issues of "young-old," "destruction-crea-tion," "masculine-feminine" and "attachment-isolation."[2] These are also related to the last two developmental stages of life identified by Erik Erikson, particularly the "crisis work" that has to be done by the individual in achieving generativity as opposed to stagnation and integrity as opposed to despair.[3]

FAITH CONCERNS OF THE YOUNG-OLD

The issue of vocation or stewardship of life is one of the primary concerns of the young-old. There are at least three special times in life when the question "what shall I do with my life" comes up: adolescence and the entry into adulthood, during the middle years as one reassesses the fulfillment of vocation in "mid-life crisis," and finally at entry into elderhood, which in our culture occurs most fre-quently with the *rite-de-passage* of retirement. Now, as one relin-quishes the full-time responsibilities and burdens of one's work, job, profession or "calling," when the course of one's income no longer depends upon daily work, the issue reasserts itself, "what shall I do with the life (years) that are left to me?" Actually, this question should be asked in the years or months preparatory to retirement. It would not be at all amiss for the pastor to consider this question with people in their very early sixties as they contemplate forthcoming retirement, for it is a theological question.

This whole process has been described by a prominent teacher of social ethics as disengagement and reengagement. Reengagement can be a kind of re-entry into the warp and woof of creative respon-sibility, of continuing participation in God's creative activity in the world. Retirement need not become a time when "you are just put up on the shelf." It is very clear to anyone who is willing to listen to people in this age cohort, that there is a continuing need and desire to be "useful," to be felt as making some kind of continuing con-tribution to society and/or the economy, to community and to the fam-ily structures. All too often in retirement it is only in the family struc-ture that there is opportunity for such a continuing contribution.

The root and ground of our vocation is Baptism. God's call to us to enter into His work of continuing creation in the world was issued to us in our baptism, and it is baptism and the baptismal faith that generates and empowers us to respond to that call. Our calling is not the service of God, however, but to the service of the neighbor. "Man is free to live according to God's will as a worker together with God in vocation, in the interest of service to the Neighbor," observes Gustav Wingren.[4] Like baptism, and its blessings, this call or vocation remains with us throughout our lifetime; there is no retirement from Christian vocation. Only death and thereby entry into the Kingdom of the Gospel brings an end to the Christian's vocation.

Our actions of caring for the neighbor are a medium of God's love for others, for the whole world. In the exercise of our vocation, we become "masks of God." In our loving actions and our service to the neighbor is hidden, or "masked," the very love of God.

The "arena" in which vocation is enacted, is the place in which we stand. The original context for this was to rebutt the medieval notion that one could best, or perhaps only, serve God by retreating from the world into some monastic hideaway. A modern counterpart of this is the notion that "vocation" has only to do with "church work." Wingren observes, "Since it is in my situation on earth that I meet my neighbor, my vocation comprehends all my relations with different neighbors; indeed my vocation can be said to consist of all those relations."[5] This understanding originates from Paul's word to the Corinthian congregation:

> Let everyone lead the life which the Lord has assigned to him, and in which God has called him . . . Everyone should remain in the state in which he was called. Were you a slave when called? (to faith in Christ), never mind . . . if you can gain your freedom, avail yourself of the opportunity. For he who was called in the Lord as a slave is a freed man of the Lord. Likewise he who was free when called is a slave of Christ . . . (1 Corinthians 7:17-22).

"There is no way to do God's will in a sinful world except as we meet the demands of our standing place" writes one noted theologian.

What this suggests for the Christian who ponders life after retirement and for the pastor who shepherds, is that there is no retreat from the world, either into monasteries or into retirement. You are still called to be involved, according to the demands of one's "place" in life, even though you have given up occupational roles, or professional roles. You are still set in a network of human relationships as friend, wife, or husband, father or mother, colleague or citizen. In those relationships, you can continue to be the channel of God's creative and redeeming love by your loving concern for the neighbor's well being.

Consideration of talent and ability in finding one's post-retirement vocation is as important as it was in adolescent years. Too often elder-vocations are not fulfilling because the elder is "underemployed," best illustrated by the congregation that utilizes the retired banker to take up the offering (because, presumably, this has something to do with finances). As one considers various volunteer opportunities with elders, the issue is not just to "fill the retiree's time" but rather to fill time and need with the talents and resources the retiree can provide.

A second principle of a biblical doctrine of vocation is that our standing before God does not depend upon how successfully we discharge our vocation in the world. This is always important, at whatever time of life, but it is of particular importance for the older person. One of the severe threats of retirement, as we have already noted, is the feeling of being "worthless" now that one is no longer economically/socially "productive." This feeling has theological dimensions as well; more than one elder feels the threat of abandonment by God now that they can no longer be "active" especially in church work. Anna, an elder who was being visited by a parish volunteer expressed this concern.

Anne:	Did the pastor send you out to see me?
Visitor:	No, he didn't. He did ask me to stop in and see you before, the first time we talked, but since then, I have just wanted to keep in touch and see how you are getting on.
Anne:	He's been out to see me, you know. I keep telling him that he needs somebody like me to talk with. Everybody needs a sounding board, you know, somebody to bounce ideas off of. And besides, I get a lot better feeling for what's happening in that church. People say things to me that he would never hear.
Visitor:	What was the pastor's response to that?
Anne:	He never really answered me. Did you ever notice how some people do that, they never answer your questions. Sometimes pastor never even

says anything. Why, the last time I was in church, that was three months ago (she is recovering from a hip operation), he didn't say anything to me. I was feeling so down in the dumps . . . so depressed that . . . well, all it would have taken was just for him to have given me a cheery word. But he didn't even seem to notice me. Not even a touch did he give me . . . I'm not sure he even saw me . . . and nobody else seemed to either.

Visitor: You must have felt that no one cared about you.

Anne: Ain't that the truth! Why, I was wondering if God cared. Sometimes he just seems to let my troubles keep stacking up. They just keep coming one after the other, and they never seem to stop, even for a little while. It seems to me that once in a while God could give me a little time just to get even with them . . . but they just keep on coming . . .

It is very difficult, especially in our culture, to overcome the idea that our importance to God depends upon our usefulness to Him. So the doctrines of grace and the promise of Baptism are the essential backdrop to the doctrine of vocation and have, therefore, special meaning to elders. How easy it is, every pastor knows, to try to engage the young elderly into one or another aspect of "church work" (usually ushering, serving on the church council, keeping the congregation's books, and sometimes teaching Sunday School) in such a way as to subtly undercut a grace-oriented doctrine of vocation. We motivate people by guilt, rather than by gratitude and a sense of stewardship, particularly when it comes to church work. We so easily make people feel that God will abandon them if they do not productively serve him. Vocation, being "called" to serve, always requires the free response of a freely-made decision to answer the call in accordance with one's holistically considered stance in life.

One of the real blessings of a sense of vocation is that it provides meaning for life. But can life have meaning without an occupational role? That is the question which plagues the young elderly. It may not be enough to simply recite to them the elements of a Christian doctrine of vocation. "How can I serve my neighbor, now that I no longer have a clear social role, limited income, a weakened body and decreasing strength . . .'' may be the question. It is at this point often, that the pastor can be an imaginative spiritual guide through the network of strengths and liabilities and assessment of existing needs outside the network of one's primary relationships, in the pursuit of a mission in life.

FAITH CONCERNS OF THE MIDDLE-ELDERLY

It may be somewhat surprising to suggest that the concern about death and dying comes to the fore during these years. Our youthful assumptions about aging would suggest that this question is put off until the very last minute, and therefore is the concern of the frail-elderly. For some it may well be, but chaplains of nursing homes which are largely populated by the frail-elderly report that this question of dying and death, and for the Christian, hope of eternal life, is wrestled with earlier and is for many, settled by the time they reach the age of 80 or so. This was the finding of Pastor Larry Trachte who conducted a research project with one hundred and two elderly residents of Iowa. Trachte found that the frequency with which people thought about death was highest in the age group of persons 71-75 (8%), second highest in the 86-90 age group (7%), and third highest in the age group 66-70 (6%).[6]

The hope of life after death in this very religious sample of persons was predictably high. Eighty-seven individuals expressed feelings that life after death was "very important or important to them." Seven others felt it was "not very important." Trachte observes that the importance of the hope for life after death actually decreases with the age of the respondents. In response to the interviewer's question, "If you had one wish, what would it be?" Sample responses related to death included, "to end soon," "to die without pain—I've had enough already," "to go to heaven," "to die while I'm asleep," "to meet my family in heaven," "early death," "that I could be loved by my family and die a pointless death." One particularly interesting finding in the Trachte study is that nursing home residents seem to think about death less than those who lived in their own homes, or lived with family, though nursing home residents were willing to talk about death in an almost "matter of fact" manner. It should be remembered, in this connection, that a much higher proportion of people over 80 are nursing home residents.

Facing the realities of death and dying is one of the most difficult tasks confronting the human being. In one sense, the whole of pastoral ministry is directed toward this end, and shepherding of people out of death into the light and life of the Gospel. Ours is the task of nurturing faith so that the dying person might through death emerge into life eternal. The advice given to homileticians can also be given to the pastoral shepherd, "preach as a dying man (woman) to dying men (woman)."[11]

As we age, each of us confronts death on two fronts: in the bereavement at the death of loved ones and in facing our own dying. Bereavement is the anticipatory echo of our own dying. What is needed as we work through these "little deaths" and face dying itself, is a theology for dying, or better yet, a faith for dying.

The ground of such faith can only be the grace of God. But for the elder this grace is the living promise, "I am with you to the end of the age." It is the fulfilled longing of aging Anna that her pastor would pay attention to her, hear her, touch her. Grace is the unbreakable covenant God has made that "there is nothing in death or life, in the realm of spirits or superhuman powers—nothing in all creation that can separate us from the love of god in Christ Jesus" (Rom. 3:38-39, NEB). Grace is far more than the "love and acceptance" of God which we enjoy feeling. For we, as fallible sin-battle-scarred elders all know there is much in our life story that could well destroy all acceptance or love, even in family or friends. How then can we trust in the image of "love and affection," even in God, given our human intellect's need to fashion God in our own image? God's durable covenant grace is God's unconditional commitment to us.

This is vital for the elder who wrestles with death. As we face dying and consider how we will act in the agonizing pain of terminal cancer, will we lose our grip on the childlike faith in God's love and mercy and feel more like Job's wife—"curse God and die"? What happens in the long hours of coma when faith along with all sentience itself is gone? What happens when, because of a stroke, no "faith-response" can be verbalized or even thought? Does the durable covenant still hold then?

If we ask older people, or for that matter almost anyone, what it is about death that is feared most, we frequently find that it is not death, but dying that is feared. In dying elders fear the pain, the collapse of self-discipline that occurs in the face of pain, and threat. Then, when we are at our most awful, will we still be respected, cared for, loved? The grace of God does speak also to this, as the synoptic's account of the agonies of the crucifixion of the Son of God make clear. He is the guarantor that we shall not be bereft in the hour of our dying.

But the elder whose grasp of faith is threatened by despair, suffering, insentience, and who is facing an increasing dearth of loving human relationships which might mirror the love of God, will wonder, does this still apply to me? Then, it is that Paul's words are so meaningful to elders:

> Have you forgotten that when we were baptized into union with Christ Jesus we were baptized into his death? By baptism we were buried with him, and lay dead, in order that as Christ was raised from the dead in the splendor of the Father, so also we might set our feet upon the new path of life. For if we become incorporate with him in a death like His, we shall also be one with him in a resurrection like his. (Rom. 6:2-5, NEB)

Baptism, the individualized sign and seal that these promises apply *to us, to me,* is the sacrament for the aged as much as of infancy.

In Trachte's study, the older person's hope in resurrection contains elements of longing for reunion with family and friends, release from suffering, just simply "sabbath rest," and finally the expectation of meeting their Savior. In these statements and similar others which every pastor who listens to elders has heard, we have the "experiential content" of eschatology. Elders are not concerned with proof of the resurrection or of the significance of resurrection for Christology. They embrace this Gospel far more intimately, "What will it be like for me"? A pastoral theology must address that, as does the apostle Paul in his letters (cf. I Cor. 15:33ff).

The New Testament doctrine of the resurrection of the body, therefore, is of primary concern to elders confronting dying. What does it promise? Will it be a body wracked with arthritis? A body minus several organs resulting from radical surgery? These are the kinds of questions many elders would like to discuss with their pastors but "are afraid to ask," (and pastors are perhaps most grateful that they do not). Theologian Hans Schwarz suggests that understanding resurrection of the body in terms of a literal bio/physical revivication raises several problems and falls short of what Scripture means.[7] Joseph Sittler in an interview at his 75th birthday comments: "I certainly do not want to continue to love the present carcass into all eternity. That is an absurd and not at all pleasant idea.''[8] And most elders would agree.

When Scripture speaks of resurrection of the body, what is meant is the resurrection of the *person*; always Scripture thinks of persons as embodied persons but as to the "shape" of the body, Scripture is silent. Here we join Sittler who further comments, "What life beyond death might be I have no notion. If all life is engendered and created by God, then that relationship will certainly not be destroyed . . . Something continues, but what that will be, I'm perfectly willing to leave in the hands of the Originator.''[9]

For the Christian, dying and the doorway of death are an entering into the sleep *with* the faithful. For the New Testament writers, there is no vacuum after death, this is not a neutral state, nor is it the fullness of resurrection which occurs "on the last day.'' With his delightful concreteness, Martin Luther once noted, "We shall sleep until he comes and knocks at the tomb and says, "Dr. Martin, get up! Then in one moment, I will get up and I will rejoice with him in eternity.''

In eternity, the "fulfillment of time'' rather than "infinite'' time, Schwarz points out, "all life impairing defects of time will be overcome, transition, suffering, decay and death are all inextricably connected with temporality and change.''[10] All and everything eternity will be is living in God's eternal presence with the saints. In this hope we can face dying, *ars moriendi.*

FACING LIVING AND DYING IN HOPE

The theologians who concern themselves with the Christian hope see this hope as having two dimensions or directions, both of which have importance for elders. Since there are not two English words for hope or for "the future'' they use two words from the Latin: *futurum* and *adventus.* Futurum means that future which grows out of the past, the accumulation of all our past experiences, memories, the accumulation of our "history.'' Involved in this future are the inevitable changes that the pilgrimage of aging brings upon us. As we consider the gains and losses of aging the accumulating years can bring a bitter harvest, but may also bring joy as we "rest from our labors'' and reap the rewards of affection from family and our grandchildren. This hope is consequential in character; it rests upon the consequences, good or ill, of our past pilgrimage extending themselves into the future. It may be described as the trajectory of our past into the days and years ahead (See I Peter, 2:3-4).

The Creator of an orderly universe has established the possibility of this cumulative future as an expression of structure and predictability in life. Elders understand and depend upon this order in planning their lives. We depend on the fact that savings laid aside in pension plans or social security will accumulate and be a dependable source of future income. Also in human relations, as parents, or family members, or even in a circle of friends, we look forward to harvesting the accumulated concern and love and care of children in our own future. But the future brings also the loss of friends and family, the "little deaths" along the pilgrimage, fear, and loneliness. So we also anticipate continued reasonable good health as the accumulation of careful attention to diet, exercise, good stewardship of physical and emotional resources, and dread the advance of disease. God is present in this future with both judgment and blessing.

But for elders, it is vital that there be more to our hope for the future than simply the projected accumulations of the past. Liberating hope lies in our anticipation of the God who is the "creator of a new heaven and a new earth" coming down the path of life to meet us, so to speak. *Adventus* is the other form of hope identified in the theologies of hope and is not bound by the accumulations of the past; this "coming hope" transcends them. Coming to us, not out of the past into the future, but from the future into the now, it offers a hope that transcends the accumulation of past mistakes, missed opportunities, lack of courage, sin. This understanding of the future is nearer to the Biblical understanding of "new" as in "new creation." It is the affirmation of I John 3:2: "Beloved . . . it does not yet appear where we shall be, but we know that when He appears (comes to meet us) we shall be like Him." We are not exclusively bound by what we have been becoming all our lives, but in the mercy of God will surmount that and will be instead, as He is. The "Kingdom" parables of Jesus hint at the shape of this advent future with their surprise endings. There is an unpredictable, unknowable quality to the resurrection ("new" creation) life elders anticipate through death.

There is both judgment and grace in this advent hope too. For the dying, entry into the presence of God brings anticipated judgment as well as promise of mercy. But there is a particular blessing to elders in this advent hope. Human hopes necessarily rest only on the trajectory of the accumulated past, since that is the only reality we as humans know. But the advent hope is God's creative breaking into, and breaking apart, the accumulations of our history with the promise of the radical new life in resurrection which is beyond our comprehension or imagination. This advent hope says that God is not bound by human history, nor our individual accumulated past.

FAITH CONCERNS OF THE FRAIL-ELDERLY

Two faith-concerns come to the fore for the frail-elderly—the paired concerns about suffering and the providence of God. To say that they are special concerns of the frail-elderly should in no sense be construed to mean that they emerge only in the very latest stage of life. But because in the later years of life illness, crippling and catastrophic illness are so much more frequent we should expect these concerns to be more poignantly present.

Dorothy Sölle, a German theologian, has looked deeply into human suffering from a pastoral-theological perspective and notes three phases of suffering: mute suffering, anguished outcry of lament, and liberation and change.[11] Mute suffering is expressed by one woman as she confesses to her pastor that she is "kind of down . . . I don't feel God has answered my prayers. I have prayed that I would go home and I'm still here . . . I feel that I have been forsaken. I think I'll just stop praying." Pain, whether physical or spiritual, particularly for the elder, isolates the sufferer from human relationships. Mute suffering expresses the isolating character of severe pain and in turn the "muteness" creates more isolation. In mute suffering all one's physical and emotional energy is consumed in fighting pain. It is as if the sufferer does not want to drag another into the mire of pain in which they struggle, perhaps remembering their own unwillingness to venture into another's suffering when they were well. So the elder especially tries to shrug off compassion or sympathy with "don't bother about me, I can take care of myself," or remains in self-isolation out of the inordinate fear of "I don't want to be a burden to someone."

As the person continues in this struggle there are three options: to become outwardly indifferent and hardened to pain and "just keep it to myself"; to become spiritually and psychologically ill in response to the burden; or to begin to reach out and work on the suffering in some creative fashion.

The antidote to this chasm of isolation is not indifference, nor a command to be compassionate; rather it is the internal personal integrity which allows the pastor to enter another's suffering and loneliness without feeling either threatened or repulsed. For the sufferer, it is a personal integrity which sustains the sense of worth and dignity even if one is the recipient of compassion or becomes the object of another's sympathy. Such integrity is in large part the product of the conviction that "we are who we are by the Grace of God"; then identity is not solely dependent upon other people's response to us. The motivation to reach out and work on the suffering in some creative fashion must come from outside the sufferer; someone must reach down into the well of loneliness and lift the sufferer out of it. This is often the ministry of the pastoral contact.

The anguished cry of lament, the second stage of suffering identified by Dorothy Sölle is the cry of the psalmist, voiced especially in the psalms of lament "hear my cry, O God, listen to my prayer. From the end of the earth I call to thee with fainting heart" (Ps. 61:1-2), or "Out of the depths have I called to thee, O Lord; Lord hear my cry" (Ps. 130:1). Over the centuries these psalms have voiced the deep anguish of elders in their suffering. The intensity of their anguish wrings the cry from their lips. It is not easily heard; we who hear it, pastors and friends, too often respond with admonition, "Don't be such a complainer!" Such an anguished cry disturbs our own equilibrium, and we would rather not hear it.

When the cry of lament does escape the lips of the aged sufferer, it often expresses that conclusion of Job's "As I have seen, those who plow iniquity and sow trouble reap the same" (Job 4:7,ff). When illness and tragedy tumble the sand castles of our lives we all have asked, "what have I done to deserve this?" or "why is God punishing me so?" For the elder who has little left in life but the accumulated memories, and now has little to look forward to but continuing suffering and loneliness, it begins to seem like the unremitting punishment of God. In those dark hours of anguish, even the most good and upright elder can remember "the sins of my youth," mortal or venial, which could deserve what is now being suffered. These bitter herbs of memory can wipe out any perception of a gracious and merciful God.

It is important that we hear the anguished lament not only as a cry of pain, and a complaint against the absent God, but also as a cry of help, an effort to establish some personal connection with someone outside the burning ring of suffering. Our response to the outcry can become a bridge of compassion which stretches across the lonely island of pain to the mainland of a caring community. How relieving it is for the sufferers to be able to put into words the pain, the anguish and the anger that suffering brings. And to have these words come from the psalms becomes powerful evidence that God is not repulsed by our anguished cries.

Once the bridge of compassion has been established the process of "co-determination" as Sölle calls it, can take place. Co-determination simply means the consideration by both sufferer and compassionate friend of the meaning and function of the suffering. We can see this process taking place in the conversation between one woman and her pastor:

Pastor:	You sense a conflict within yourself between a faith which wants to believe in God's love for you, but you doubt whether God is really as active in delivering you as He could be?
Woman:	Yes, that's how I feel, and I don't know if I should really be feeling that way at all . . . Do you suppose that God could be working through me even as I am expressing these doubts that things don't somehow add up?
Pastor:	In your suffering you think that you might have an opportunity to respond to God . . .
Woman:	Well, I've always believed that God is never far from me . . . He is always with those who believe. But I guess I've never actually applied what that means . . . then God is actually present with me, even when I think he might not be?

If we rely only upon our own inner reflections to find the meaning of life, we will be disappointed. Viktor Frankl who discovered the tremendous importance of meaning to suffering contends that true meaning of life (and suffering) is to be found in the world rather than within the person.[12] Biblically oriented people contend that such meaning can come through God's revelation in His Word. In reaching out and engaging with another in this "co-determination" the sufferer is doing more than mere passive "accepting" of the suffering. He is trying, with the help of another to see how suffering can be used. It is to see suffering as "labor pains" as Dorothy Sölle puts it, giving birth to a larger reality of meaning and relationship.

So the question arising out of suffering changes from *"why* me, God?'' to *"how,* O Lord can this, even this, bitter anguish, be used?''

From this "co-determination" or collaborative work in suffering emerges the stage of liberation and change which Solle identifies. As communication occurs, the pain and anguish of suffering is shared, the possibility of liberation occurs, even though the "why" question is not answered.

The pastoral task with those who suffer may then be to explore how the suffering can be used to produce character and finally hope. There are also other uses to which suffering can be put, which every visitor to suffering elders has discovered. One of the students who interviewed elders in Trachte's study expressed her own reactions to conversing with her 86-year-old elder:

> She certainly has a strong faith in the Lord. Was not afraid to talk about death and dying. A very inspirational lady. I really enjoyed going and talking to this woman . . . she brightened up my life and was an inspiration to my faith.[13]

It is very important, though, that whatever use is found for suffering, that it be discovered by the elder, not imposed upon her or him. Teaching in the sense of "instruction" here can easily become callous insensitivity. Varied uses to suffering can be found, and they will vary with the life and situation of each individual person.

THE PROVIDENCE OF GOD

Though we may deal with suffering by finding how it may be used, the "why" question of suffering will not go away. There is a great need in the human spirit to find out the reason for our suffering; we can be grateful for this, for on at least the medical front this quest fuels the continuing discovery of medical procedures, drugs, etc., which bring comfort to many a sufferer.

Mrs. Sanders, who is 63, is in the hospital for possible cancer of the left ovary. Exploratory surgery is to take place later in the day, after this conversation took place. The surgery which had been scheduled for early in the morning has been delayed, and Mrs. Sanders is explaining, "I'm a little depressed. I was supposed to go to surgery today, I was all ready to go at 9:30 and they came and

told me it had been cancelled . . . they found something in one of
the tests on my lung so they didn't want to operate until they know
what is wrong."

Mrs. Sanders continues a bit later in the conversation, "I'm still
looking at this positively. I wasn't scared when I came in and I'm
not scared now. I have a positive attitude. The doctor operated on
me 20 years ago and did a good job, I have confidence in him . . . I
told him I put God first and me second and him third. And as long as
he does what God wills, everything will be okay . . . "

Chaplain:	God is with you and I'm sure he is guiding the doctors.
Mrs. Sanders:	That's right. God calls his own to him when it's time. But (she pauses . . .) I don't think it's my turn yet. I'm thinking positively and I'm not afraid because I know God is taking care of me.
Chaplain:	Your faith is very strong.
Mrs. Sanders:	I know my life is in God's hands.

Here we have a fairly typical expression of a belief that is of great
importance to older people; confidence in the Providence of God.
What is particularly agonizing about suffering which generates the
"Why, O God, is this happening to me?" question is the fear that
somehow the suffering is evidence that one is no longer in God's
care. It may well be that the desired answer to this question is not, as
we pastors so often think, an explanation of why suffering does not
mean that the questioner has fallen out of favor and is no longer
under the care of God.

Mrs. Sanders can face a fearful operation with considerable calm
because she is confident that this, too, is under the providential care
of God. Her life, as she puts it, "is in God's hands." Confidence
that this is true may very well be the reason why the very old have
less concern or fear of death. This particular perspective, the providential care of God, is one of the most vital for older people, and a
key pastoral task is the careful development of this faith.

The transcendence of God does not mean indifference to our
need. Because God is "beyond" everything, "above it" so to
speak, He can also be "in" everything. So, as James Robinson put
it, "God is in the cancer as he is in the sunset, and he is to be met
and responded to in each . . . " The ancient Jewish philosopher

Maimonedes kept reminding his followers, "His power *is* His goodness, which in turn *is* the infallibility of His will."[14]

What the biblical faith asserts is that through all the processes of life and history, there is a personal outcome to be faced and a love to be met which nothing, finally, can defeat. This is the faith of Paul (Romans 8:28). It is more than the faith that all things work together for good, more than the conviction or hope that God will make everything turn out all right in the end. It is the trust that in everything, no matter what its cause or why it happened, He (the Spirit) works in us for good as we love God (Romans 8). For those who respond and trust in love in any and all circumstances, no matter how pointless, there is to be met in the event itself, the graciousness of a Father, capable of transforming and liberating even the most baffling events into some meaning and purpose.

LIFE REVIEW AND PROVIDENCE

Almost never do we "see the will of God" in any direct way. It is like standing on the bow of an ocean liner in the middle of the ocean. Standing on the bow, looking ahead will not tell you the direction of the ship. But move to the stern, see the pattern of the wake, where you have been, and you discover the course of the ship. So one discovers the providential care of God, by looking at the wake of our lives. There is a biblical term, that describes this process: "anamnesis" which is the remembering of the past events of God's guidance. But it is not merely a mental recall; for ancient people of God and for the New Testament church, anamnesis was the occasion for replicating, bringing back to life the experience recalled. For the ancient Hebrews to "remember" a name of the person was to immediately call forth the soul that the name designated; there is this quality about our remembering the names of family members and friends whom we have lost in death. Again and again as Israel was at a critical point in its history it was called upon to remember the deliverance of God. So was the guidance of God not only brought to mind, but brought into living action at the moment of remembering.

The process of "life review" is strongly recommended as an important way of developing on one's life. A life review is like looking at the wake of our life—and seeing the direction of God's guiding, caring nurture as He was at the helm of the ship of our life. Even if life was bitter, there is evidence that at significant turning points, through little decisions, apparent coincidences, we are led. The loving presence of God was there even in suffering. Such a life review can do much to counter that compelling fear of old age, "when I am no longer active, effective, or useful, will God abandon me?"

Stimulating and guiding anamnesis or "life review" can be one of the most important pastoral contributions a minister can make for the ongoing life of the elderly, particularly the frail-elderly. Creative remembering which recalls the moments of God's guidance, the occasions of joy and love in life, the momentous occasions of decision, can be important in recreating the person of someone who fears abandonment by God and all others. Truly helpful is that life review which concludes, "O God, our help in ages past, Our help for years to come!" Out of this grows both trust in the past and hope and courage for the future.

NOTES

1. Pruyser, Paul. *The Minister as Diagnostician.* (Philadelphia: Westminster Press), 1976.

2. Levinson, Daniel J., et al. *The Seasons of a Man's Life.* (New York: Alfred Knopf), 1978.

3. Erikson, Erik. *Childhood and Society.* (New York: Norton Publishing Co.), 1964.

4. Wingren, Gustav. *Luther on Vocation.* (Philadelphia: Muhlenberg Press), 1957. p. 65.

5. Ibid., p. 65.

6. Trachte, Larry. *The Meaning of Aging: Viktor Frankl's Logotherapy and the Elderly.* (Iowa City: State University of Iowa), Unpublished Master Thesis, 1982.

7. Schwarz, Hans. *On the Way to the Future.* (Minneapolis: Augsburg Publishing House), 1979, p. 185.

8. Sittler, Joseph. Personal Communication, September, 1984.

9. Ibid.

10. Schwarz, op. cit.

11. Sölle, Dorothy, *Suffering* (trans. by E. R. Kalin). (Philadelphia: Fortress Press), 1975.

12. Frankl, Victor. *The Will to Meaning.* (New York: New American Library), 1969.

13. Trachte, op. cit.

14. Robinson, J. T. *Exploration into God.* (Stanford, CA: Stanford University Press), 1967.

The Attitudes and Knowledge of Church Members and Pastors Related to Older Adults and Retirement

Mary Dean Apel, Ph.D.

ABSTRACT. The attitudes and knowledge of 260 church members and pastors, aged 21-94, related to older adults and retirement were studied. Data obtained from mailed questionnaires were examined and statistically analyzed to determine: (1) attitudes and knowledge; (2) differences in attitudes and knowledge among demographic groups; and (3) differences between church members' and pastors' attitudes and knowledge.

Attitudes were generally positive and differed significantly when respondents were grouped by age, education, income, health status, marital status, the number of living parents and church involvement. There were no significant differences when respondents were grouped by sex and the number of living children. Subjects believe they have only some knowledge related to the areas included in the questionnaire and differed significantly when grouped by the demographic variables excepting sex. There were significant differences between the attitudes and knowledge of church members and pastors.

Findings indicate a need for (1) lifespan learning experiences related to personal adjustment, social relationships, health care and maintenance and economic planning, (2) opportunity for increased intergenerational relationships, and (3) pre-retirement planning.

INTRODUCTION

The majority of the 35 million Americans who are expected to be 65 years of age or older by the year 2000 will be well, active and striving to remain contributing members of our society. Negative attitudes and lack of knowledge related to aging and the retirement

Mary Dean Apel, 1816 Virginia Dr., Manhattan, Kansas 66502.

31

years may impede progress towards that goal. Lifespan learning concerning aging and retirement and increased intergenerational opportunities would promote positive attitudes and encourage continuing growth and development throughout life.

Studying the characteristics of the aged has been the primary focus of efforts to discover the issues associated with aging. Most people still do not accept the concept of "normal aging" (Woodruff and Birren, 1975). "The rest of us, not the old, determine the status and position of the old person in the social order" (Rosow, 1962, p. 191). Therefore, it is necessary to consider the attitude of the rest of society toward the aged and toward the process of aging (Levin and Levin, p. 63, 1980).

Most older people feel their life is better than the general public believes it to be; older adults wish to be productive and can be so (Harris and Associates, 1975). Negative attitudes of the aged disappear when older adults are educated, affluent and healthy; they feel that activity is the key to happiness (Hellebrandt, 1980). Despite age stereotypes some older people prefer to work past the age of 65 (Billings, 1980). However, many workers wish to retire before the mandatory age (Foner and Schwab, 1981). Health status and preretirement feelings about retirement are more significant predictors of retirement attitudes and satisfaction than the voluntary/nonvoluntary decision (Kimmel, 1978). Others cite economic conditions and emotional concerns as sources of dissatisfaction in retirement and interpersonal relations as a primary source of satisfaction.

Research to determine what knowledge people have concerning the aging process and behaviors resulting from that knowledge is not available. Studies investigating the attitudes and knowledge related to older adults and retirement among all ages of church members and pastors were not found.

METHODOLOGY

The hypotheses for this research called for an investigation of church members' attitudes and knowledge related to older adults and retirement when they were grouped according to demographic variables, and a comparison of church members and pastors attitudes and knowledge. Demographic variables selected by the researcher and scales developed by V. L. Boyack and D. M. Tiberi (1982) were organized into a questionnaire which was mailed to a random sample of church members.

The demographic variables included age, sex, income, years of education, perceived health status, family structure (marital status, number of living parents, number of living children) and church involvement (regularity of church attendance, number of church positions or offices held, number of church organizations to which members belonged). Subjects' preference for ages to include in church activities they attended was included to obtain an indication of the possibilities for intergenerational relationships.

Scales to measure attitudes included: (1) a semantic differential scale of 12 pairs of words to measure attitudes towards retirement and (2) Likert scales including 15 statements to measure attitudes related to resistance to retirement, functional worth and capability in retired persons, perceived zest in retirement, and vulnerability to depression in retirement. Scale choices were: strongly agree, agree, undecided, disagree, and strongly disagree. Likert scales to measure perceived knowledge included 26 statements related to personal adjustment, health care and maintenance, economic planning, and social relationships. Scale choices were very knowledgeable, knowledgeable, some knowledge, a little knowledge, and no knowledge. Responses were coded so that the highest mean scores would indicate positive attitudes and the most knowledge.

The researcher explained the need for the study to pastors and delegates from 25 Lutheran congregations at a regional meeting. A follow-up letter requesting the names of church members who were 21 years of age and older, soliciting questions and concerns, explaining procedures for collecting data, and proposing another personal contact at a Synod convention was sent to each pastor. A 15 percent random sample of names was selected from each of the 21 church lists received. The sample included 421 members and the 15 pastors of those churches. The four churches not choosing to participate have profiles similar to the participating churches.

At the Synod convention each of the 15 pastors received (1) cover letters explaining the need for the study, assuring subjects of confidentiality and outlining procedures to follow; (2) questionnaires; (3) self addressed stamped envelopes for returning the questionnaires to the church; (4) the names of the individuals to receive questionnaires; (5) postage for mailing the questionnaires to the subjects; (6) a self addressed stamped packet for returning the questionnaires to the researcher; and (7) procedures for mailing and collecting the questionnaires.

Each pastor signed a cover letter that had already been signed by the researcher; he then placed the cover letter, a questionnaire, and return envelope in a church envelope and mailed them from his church. If an individual had not returned the questionnaire by the suggested due date the pastor contacted that individual to encourage an immediate response. One week after that contact the pastor mailed the questionnaires received to the researcher.

Analysis of variance and the t-test were used to test for significant differences ($p < .05$) among and between mean scores. The Scheffe procedure indicated which groups were significantly different ($p < .05$) from other groups. The homogeneity of variances identified in the data and the reliability coefficients on the scales added strength to the research.

RESULTS

The population studied comprised an older group; 30% were over 65 years of age and 7% were 80-94 years of age. Half have formal education beyond high school although 9% had not attended high school. Almost one-third have yearly incomes under $10,000 with half having yearly incomes between $10,000 and $30,000. Three-fourths believe they have good health. The majority are married and have one or more living children. About half have one or two living parents. Most members attend church regularly (61% attend once or twice a week); 54% hold church leadership roles and 61% are members of one or more church organizations. Church members (69%) report they like to participate in some church activities for people of all ages.

Pastors and members had generally positive attitudes related to retirement; they believe retirement is happy, good, active, and full. Some believe their retirement is unplanned. As indicated in Table 1 those aged 56-70, or those with yearly incomes over $30,000, good health, or active church participation had significantly more positive attitudes than those aged 71-94, or those with yearly incomes under $10,000, fair to poor health, or less active church participation.

Pastors and members had generally positive attitudes concerning functional worth and capability in retired persons, resistance to retirement, perceived zest in retirement, and vulnerability to depression in retirement. They agreed that older people are valuable because of their experience, are just as valuable to society as younger people, and can learn things just as well as younger people. They disagreed that retirement means not doing much of anything

Table 1

Significant Differences Indicated on the Retirement Scale

Variable	Group with the Highest Mean Score	ANOVA - F or t-test - t	Group with the Lowest Mean Score
Age	56-70 6.0028	.0054a	71-94 5.2544
Annual Income	Over $30,000 6.1319	.0086a	Under $10,000 5.4640
Health	Good 5.9994	.0002	Fair or poor 5.2948
Church:			
Attendance	Once or twice a week 5.9883	.0047a	Rarely or not at all 4.9444
Positions or Offices	One 6.1012	.0038a	None 5.6135
Age Preference for Activities Attended	All Ages 6.0236	.0146	Own age group 4.9583

Note. High scores indicate positive attitudes. Maximum score=7. p<.05.
aThe Scheffé procedure indicates significant comparisons between means.

and that older people should not exercise when they do not have to do so. Findings reported in Table 2 indicate those under age 55, or those with more than a high school education, yearly incomes over $30,000, good health, spouses, living parents, or active church participation have the most positive attitudes.

Church members and pastors believe they have only some knowledge concerning health care and maintenance, social relationships, economic planning, and personal adjustment. As indicated in Table 3 those aged 71-94 or those with no living parents indicate significantly more knowledge about health care services than those aged 21-55 or those with two living parents. Table 3 also indicates that those aged 56-70, or those married, or those with no living parents, or active church participation indicate significantly more knowledge related to health maintenance than those aged 21-40, or those single, those with two living parents, or less active church participation.

Table 2

Significant Differences Indicated on the Attitude Scales

Variable	Group with the Highest Mean Score	ANOVA - F or t-test - t	Group with the Lowest Mean Score

Functional Worth and Capability in Retired Persons

Variable	Group with the Highest Mean Score	ANOVA - F or t-test - t	Group with the Lowest Mean Score
Age	21-55 3.7553	.0000a	71-94 3.1515
Formal Education	More than high school 3.7684	.0000a	High school or less 3.4072
Annual Income	Over $30,000 3.7128	.0070a	Under $10,000 3.3724
Health	Good 3.6543	.0002	Fair or poor 3.3130
Marital Status	Married 3.6327	.0325a	Widowed or Divorced 3.3636
Number of Living Parents	Two 3.7790	.0003a	None 3.4429
Church: Positions or Offices	One 3.6734	.0345	None 3.4772
Groups Belonged To	Five or more 3.8588	.0422a	None 3.5079
Age Preference for Activities Attended	Some with own age group and some with all ages 3.6790	.0005a	Makes no difference 3.3387

Resistance to Retirement

Variable	Group with the Highest Mean Score	ANOVA - F or t-test - t	Group with the Lowest Mean Score
Church Attendance	Once or twice a week 3.7131	.0166	Rarely or not at all 3.3636

Perceived Zest in Retirement

Variable	Group with the Highest Mean Score	ANOVA - F or t-test - t	Group with the Lowest Mean Score
Formal Education	College 3.4250	.0140a	High school or less 3.1402
Health	Good 3.3144	.0078	Fair or poor 3.3085

Table 2 continued

Variable	Group with the Highest Mean Score	ANOVA - F or t-test t	Group with the Lowest Mean Score
	Vulnerability to Depression in Retirement		
Age	41-55 4.3571	.0002a	56-94 3.9375
Formal Education	More than College 4.3302	.0066a	High school or less 4.0160
Health	Good 4.1923	.0047	Fair or poor 3.9151
Number of Living Parents	Two 4.3092	.0069a	None 4.0198
Church: Positions or Offices	One 4.2470	.0216a	None 4.0091
Organizations Belonged To	Five or more 4.4429	.0077a	None 3.9837

Note. High scores indicate positive attitudes. Maximum score=5. p<.05
aThe Scheffe procedure indicates significant comparisons between means.

Table 3

Significant Differences Indicated on the Perceived Knowledge Scales

Variable	Group with the Highest Mean Score	ANOVA - F or t-test - t	Group with the Lowest Mean Score
	Health Care		
Age	71-94 2.9191	.0000a	41-55 1.9235
Number of Living Parents	None 2.7076	.0000a	Two 1.7796
	Health Maintenance		
Age	56-70 3.4467	.0013a	21-40 2.9077
Marital Status	Married 3.2450	.0124a	Single 2.3000

Table 3 continued

Health Maintenance

Number of Living Parents	None 3.4314	.0049a	Two 2.9973
Church: Attendance	Once or twice a week 3.3290	.0142a	Once or twice a year 2.6526
Age Preference for Activities Attended	Some with own age group and some with all ages 3.4745	.0159a	Makes no difference 2.9731

Social Relationships

Marital Status	Married, widowed or divorced 2.6975	.0015a	Single 1.4440
Number of Living Children	Three 2.8333	.0017a	None 1.8667

Economic Planning

Age	56-70 3.1050	.0286a	21-40 2.6831
Income	Over $50,000 3.6667	.0145a	Under $10,000 2.6667
Health	Good 2.9429	.0422	Fair or poor 2.6413
Church Attendance	Once or twice a week 3.0084	.0074a	Once or twice a year 2.4015

Personal Adjustment

Age	41-55 3.2781	.0057a	71-94 2.7661
Formal Education	More than college 3.3726	.0058a	High school or less 3.0109
Health	Good 3.2230	.0007	Fair or poor 2.8404

Table 3 continued

Variable	Group with the Highest Mean Score	ANOVA - F or t-test - t	Group with the Lowest Mean Score

----

Personal Adjustment

Church:

Attendance	Once or twice a week 3.2412	.0066a	Once or twice a year 2.6989
Positions or Offices	Two or more 3.2525	.0476	None 3.0204
Groups Belonged To	Five or more 3.4679	.0159	One 2.9618

Note. High scores indicate positive attitudes. Maximum score=5. $p<.05$.
aThe Scheffé procedure indicates significant comparisons between means.

Table 3 reports that those who were married, widowed or divorced, or had three living children indicate significantly more knowledge concerning social relationships than those who were single, or had no children.

Church members and pastors believe they are knowledgeable about the consequences of not making a will but have little knowledge regarding where to find help in coping with problems; how to estimate the amount of Social Security received; and finding employment when retired. Findings reported in Table 3 indicate that those aged 56-70, or those with yearly incomes over $50,000, good health, or regular church attendance indicate significantly more knowledge concerning economic planning than those aged 21-40, or those with yearly incomes under $10,000, fair or poor health, or with less regular church attendance.

Church members and pastors believe they have some knowledge of how to plan leisure time, but believe they have little knowledge regarding how to deal with loneliness, and how to be more sensitive and aware of their own changing needs. Table 3 indicates that those aged 41-55, or those with more than a college education, good health, or active church participation indicate significantly more knowledge concerning personal adjustment than those aged 71-94, or those with a high school education or less, fair or poor health, or less active church participation.

The attitudes and knowledge of pastors and church members differ significantly in regard to older adults and retirement. Table 3 indicates that pastors' attitudes regarding the functional worth and capability of retired persons and vulnerability to depression in retirement are more positive than church members'. Pastors indicate significantly more perceived knowledge related to personal adjustment, economic planning, and social relationships while church members indicate significantly more perceived knowledge related to health care. (See Table 4.)

WHAT CAN THE CHURCH DO?

Education for aging is essential for church members and pastors. This research indicates they believe they have only some knowledge regarding (1) the importance of being involved in pre-retirement planning and life span learning experiences, (2) dealing with loneliness, (3) being more aware and sensitive of their changing needs through the life cycle, (4) planning for increasing health care costs and adequate retirement income, and (5) initiating and establishing positive social relationships with family members and others of all ages.

Churches can provide opportunities for adult church members to understand the aging process and what they can do to continue positive growth and development throughout life. Not only does the church offer an environment conducive to learning but in many cases resources for planning, information, teaching, and sharing are available in the congregation. Opportunities to learn in church services, organization meetings and special study groups would help all ages to gain new knowledge, understand one another and share knowledge. Church members aged 56-70, who have the most positive attitudes towards retirement, could be facilitators for retirement study groups. Pastors who have greater understanding of the value and capabilities of older adults could share their knowledge. Those who have experienced the impact of prolonged illness, widowhood, retirement and inadequate resources can share with each other and with those who have not had such experiences.

Intergenerational activities will show children that aging is a natural developmental stage and promote positive attitudes about aging in all age groups. Findings in this study indicate that those who prefer attending activities including all age groups have positive attitudes related to older adults and retirement. Churches include

Table 4

Significant Differences Indicated in the Attitudes and Perceived Knowledge
of Church Members and Pastors

Scale	Group with the Highest Mean Score	t-test - t	Group with the Lowest Mean Score
Functional Worth and Capability in Retired Persons[a]	Pastors 3.8667	.0260	Members 3.560
Vulnerability to Depression in Retirement[a]	Pastors 4.5000	.0150	Members 4.1094
Personal Adjustment[b]	Pastors 3.6161	.0000	Members 3.1177
Health Care[b]	Members 2.3289	.0350	Pastors 1.7321
Economic Planning[b]	Pastors 3.2738	.0210	Members 2.8584
Social Relationships[b]	Pastors 3.1429	.0060	Members 2.5534

Note. High scores indicate positive attitudes. Maximum score=5. p<.05.
[a]Attitude Scale
[b]Knowledge Scale

families, children, and older adults. This reality makes it possible to initiate natural and constructive interactions between generations, encourage older adult participation and leadership in all facets of church life and plan programs and events to integrate all ages.

Care and services for those in need, or for families who are caring for them, will remain a vital task. The population studied comprised an older group. Other church populations indicate similar profiles. Adult children who feel responsible for dependent parents express concern about this role. "Educational programs which specify and demonstrate appropriate supportive behaviors in the provision of filial care for an increasingly dependent elderly parent could help both men and women by promoting realistic assessments of the filial responsibility commitment, and by allaying fears which stem from feelings of inadequacy and helplessness" (Levande, p. 313, 1980). The ability of family members to view dependency as normal and acceptable is a strength for both nuclear and generational families.

Churches can provide respite for family members who are caring for older parents; they can make it possible for those who cannot attend church, not only to hear the Word but to continue witnessing to others; and they can offer companionship, friendship and consolation. The church must be physically accessible, provide needed transportation, and plan worship services considering the length of the service, hearing or sight deficiencies, and familiarity with the liturgy. Creative ways to continue the church involvement of adults who cannot attend church services would improve their life satisfaction.

Churches can help to identify older adults who are truly needy and put them in touch with agencies who provide services. They could provide test models for housing resources such as share-a-home, day care, granny annexes, and others. Some churches are establishing Day Centers for older adults at the church.

Church advocacy for older adults can help to maintain their sense of worth and promote continued social services and programs. Churches could be the one place to offer guidance and support to those facing the multiple facets of the health care network. Agencies seem to provide better services if someone, such as the church, expresses a special interest.

Older adults are expected to be physically and mentally vigorous into their 70's. The age cohort who will be 50-75 in the year 2000 will be searching for new roles. Churches could develop programs to generate new interests and enthusiasms among this age group to carry over into the 70's and to promote new goals such as part-time work, volunteer work, or other activities. Church advocacy can influence society's efforts to provide opportunities and resources for older adults.

CONCLUSION

National church bodies, church colleges, universities and seminaries, regional offices, and local parishes can work together to promote research, identify needs, provide appropriate education for pastors, and initiate opportunities for church members, young and old alike, to learn about aging and the retirement years. Most churches are involved in programs for the elderly. Much of what can be done to prepare all ages for older adulthood will depend on specific church situations and the creativity and enthusiasm of pastors and church leaders. As we live we age. As we are aging we live. Churches can play an important role in supplying information and programs that will enable adults to make their living and aging a joy.

REFERENCES

Billings, A. E.; and Others (1980). *Older Americans: A Review of Issues and Their Implications.* Material made available at The White House Conference on Aging (3rd, Washington, D. C., November 30-December 3, 1981). Hartford, CT.: Travelers Insurance Co.

Boyack, L. L. and Tiberi, D.M. (1982). Preretirement Scale. In Mangen and Peterson, *Social Roles and Social Participation*, (pp. 242-245 and 266-271). Minneapolis: University of Minnesota Press.

Foner, Anne and Schwab, Karen (1981). *Aging and Retirement.* Belmont, CA.: Wadsworth, Inc.

Harris, Louis and Associates, Inc. (1975). *The Myth and Reality of Aging in America.* Washington, D. C.: National Council on the Aging, Inc.

Hellebrandt, Frances A. (1980). Aging Among the Advantaged: A New Look at the Stereotypes of the Elderly. *Gerontologist, 20*(4), 404-417.

Kimmel, Douglas C.; and Others (1978). Retirement Choice and Retirement Satisfaction. *Journal of Gerontology, 33*(4), 574-578.

Levande, Diane I. (1980). Filial responsibility and caretaker selection. In N. Stinnett, B. Chesser, J. Defrain and P. Knaub (Eds.), *Family Strengths* (pp. 305-317). Lincoln, NE: University of Nebraska Press.

Levin, J. and Levin, W. C. (1980). *Ageism.* Belmont, CA.: Wadsworth Publishing Co.

Rosow, Irving (1962). Old Age: One Moral Dilemma of an Affluent Society. *Gerontologist, 2*, 182-195.

Woodruff, D. and Birren, J. (1975). *Aging-Scientific Perspectives and Social Issues.* New York: D. Van Nostrand Co.

How to Assimilate the Elderly Into Your Parish: The Effects of Alienation on Church Attendance

Rev. Douglas E. Fountain

ABSTRACT. This research is a scientific study of retired persons, to attempt to determine why they drop out of the church upon reaching retirement age. The hypothesis is that a person drops out of active church life because he/she feels alienated within the social system known as the church.

Groups were tested in Michigan, Indiana, and Florida. Each group was tested for church attendance, religiosity, alienation and religious experience. Using alienation as the independent variable, it was determined that there was a correlation between alienation and church attendance. These two variables were found to be correlated at the 0.001 level of confidence. Upon further examination it was found that the computed T-Statistic indicated that the correlation was inverse in nature. As alienation increases, church attendance measurably decreases.

Due to the findings of this research the hypothesis was accepted.

Having determined that alienation is a primary cause of decline in church attendance among the elderly, ways in which to decrease alienation and therefore increase church attendance are presented. A primary agent in the process of reducing alienation is psycho-social bonding and ways to increase the bonding process are discussed. Bonding is that process by which a person attaches to, and makes a social connection with another person. The bond that is formed is often difficult to eradicate. Alienation could be described as a state of being bondless within a social system.

INTRODUCTION

Two assumptions made by leaders of the church are (1) if a person is "religious," he/she will worship and (2) as people get older, they tend to increase their church attendance, barring illness. The

Rev. Douglas E. Fountain is Pastor, Epiphany Lutheran Church, Lake Worth, Florida. His address is Epiphany Lutheran Church, 4460 Jubilee Rd., Lake Worth, Florida 33467.

research presented challenges those long held beliefs and leads us to believe that there are other factors more powerful in determining church attendance.

Consider this: A man and his wife retire and move to Florida. For decades, the church has had a central place in their lives. They may have been members of one congregation for 20, 30, or even 50 years. Now they leave it. They grieve the loss of so many friends and relatives at one time. The relationships that death has not ended now are, for all intents and purposes, ended. They try to find a new church in Florida, but no matter how hard they try, it just is not "home" to them. They feel lost in the new surroundings. To make matters worse, age has taken its toll—they can not see or hear or get around so well anymore. The familiar old Lutheran Hymnal has been replaced by The Lutheran Worship or The Lutheran Book of Worship. The pastor in the pulpit is a blur and they have trouble making out what he is saying. What was meant to be a meaningful religious experience has become a nightmare. So they stay home, watch television preachers and read Portals of Prayer, Guideposts, or whatever they can find. Is it any wonder that this couple has dropped out of the church? This couple is suffering the effects of alienation within the social system known as the church.

RESEARCH DATA

A. Sample Description

The total population of the research sample is 108, of which 70 are female and 38 are male. All are retired between the ages of 65 and 94. Sixty persons are Lutheran, 43 are Roman Catholic, 3 are Methodist, and 2 are Presbyterian. This sample was drawn from three different geographical areas: Michigan, Indiana, and Florida. The sample was randomly selected as follows:

The first group was selected at a retirement village located at Oveido, Florida. The group selected was a group of people living independently in duplexes. They had full mobility and could travel to various churches at will. There is a Lutheran Church located about 1/2 mile from the duplex neighborhood. Most residents use this facility, however, the church is not made up primarily of residents of this village. The church serves the entire town of Oveido and smaller surrounding areas.

The second group was located at Lutheran Homes Inc. at Fort Wayne, Indiana. The residents live in an independent housing facility at Lutheran Homes known as Concord Village. Residents lived independently in their own apartments. Most residents of this home were from the Fort Wayne area and preferred to worship in their home congregations.

The third group was located in Southgate, Michigan, and was part of the Southgate Seniors Association. The first two groups were made up entirely of Lutherans and it was felt that if this research were to have application to populations other than Lutherans, other religious backgrounds must be included in the study. The Southgate Seniors Association is a group that is sponsored by the City of Southgate, Michigan. Members of the association were made up of the general population of the city, and therefore other religions were represented. This group was made up of persons over the age of 65 who had full mobility and worshipped in their own various churches.

B. Questionnaire Description

Due to the nature of this population, an attempt was made to keep the questionnaire as simple as possible. The test instrument was made up of two pre-tested questionnaires that have high degrees of validity and reliability. The alienation scale is titled "Alienation Within a Social System" (Shaw and Wright, 1971). The second scale is titled "Dimensions of Religiosity" (King and Hunt, 1969).

ANALYSIS OF DATA

All analysis of the collected data was completed by computer. Table 1 gives the mean, range, standard deviation, median, mode, variance and maximum score for each of the tested variables of alienation, religiosity, church experience and church attendance.

The purpose of this project was to determine whether alienation has an influence on church attendance and for that reason alienation was selected as the dependent variable, with the other three fields as independent variables.

In the cross tabulations which were constructed for the Chi-Square computations the only cross tab that was significant was Alienation and Church Attendance. The cross tab yields a Chi-

Table 1 -- Data for Tested Variables of Alienation, Religiosity, Church Experience and Church Attendance

VARIABLE 1: ALIENATION

MEAN	=	10.17593	MEDIAN	=	10.00000	RANGE	=	13.00000
STDEV	=	2.720053	MODE	=	10.00000	MAXIMUM	=	16.00000
MINIMUM	=	3.000000	VARIANCE	=	7.398692		

SAMPLE SIZE = 108

VARIABLE 2: RELIGIOSITY

MEAN	=	13.54815	MEDIAN	=	14.00000	RANGE	=	6.000000
STDEV	=	.9304446	MODE	=	14.00000	MAXIMUM	=	14.00000
MINIMUM	=	8.000000	VARIANCE	=	.8657272		

SAMPLE SIZE = 108

VARIABLE 3: EXPERIENCE

MEAN	=	16.57407	MEDIAN	=	17.00000	RANGE	=	14.00000
STDEV	=	3.186509	MODE	MORE....		MAXIMUM	=	21.00000
MINIMUM	=	7.000000	VARIANCE	=	10.15384		

SAMPLE SIZE = 108

VARIABLE 4: ATTENDANCE

MEAN	=	9.351851	MEDIAN	=	9.000000	RANGE	=	13.00000
STDEV	=	2.888513	MODE	=	10.00000	MAXIMUM	=	13.00000
MINIMUM	=	.0000000	VARIANCE	=	8.342362		

SAMPLE SIZE = 108

Square of 21.250 with four degrees of freedom. This is significant at the .001 level of confidence. This test indicates that if a person feels alienated within the church then his/her church attendance will be affected. Table 2 presents the complete breakdown of the Chi-Square for these variables.

Inasmuch as Chi-Square only shows correlation, Multiple Regression Analysis was completed to determine the exact way in which the variables are correlated. Church Attendance was used as the dependent variable and Alienation was variable 1, Religiosity variable 2, and Religious Experience as variable 3 (see Table 3). The computed T-Statistic was − 3.1988. This is significant at the 0.05 level of confidence. This statistic demonstrates that the two variables of Alienation and Church Attendance are correlated in a negative manner. In other words, as alienation is increased, church attendance correspondingly decreases.

With the foregoing information we can accept the hypothesis that states, "Regardless of a persons religiosity, or the persons positive religious experience, if the person becomes alienated within the

```
Table 2 -- Cross Tabulation of
Attendance by Alienation
              ATTENDANCE
                LOW        8--      HIGH     TOTAL
ALIENATION                  12
           I---------I--------I--------I
     LOW I      1 I      2 I      2 I       5
         I   29.0 I   40.0 I   40.0 I     7.2
         I    8.3 I    3.7 I   66.7 I
         I    1.4 I    2.9 I    2.9 I
         I---------I--------I--------I
     8-12 I      6 I     42 I      0 I      48
         I   12.5 I   87.5 I     .0 I    69.6
         I   50.0 I   77.8 I     .0 I
         I    8.7 I   60.9 I     .0 I
         I---------I--------I--------I
    HIGH I      5 I     10 I      1 I      16
         I   31.3 I   62.5 I    6.3 I    23.2
         I   41.7 I   18.5 I   33.3 I
         I    7.2 I   14.5 I    1.4 I
         I---------I--------I--------I
   TOTAL       12       54       3        69
              17.4     78.3     4.3    100.0
```

Table 3 -- Multiple Regression Analysis for Alienation, Religiosity, and Religious Experience, with Church Attendance as the Dependent Variable

VARIABLE NO.	MEAN	STD. DEV.	CORRELATION X VS Y	REGRESSION COEFF.	STD. ERROR OF REG.COEF.	COMPUTED T VALUE
1	10.176	2.7200	-.2911	-.3034028	.0948	-3.1798
2	13.648	.9304	.2273	.4911763	.2962	1.6584
3	16.574	3.1864	.2622	.1795841	.0865	2.0757
DEPENDENT						
4	9.352	2.8883				

social system known as the church, his or her church attendance will decrease and possibly even stop.''

BARRIERS TO AFFILIATION

As a group, the elderly are prime candidates for alienation within the church. Why? As the earlier example illustrated, there is no single, simple answer to that question.

First, there are physical barriers. Of those persons tested, 98 percent indicated some type of physical impairment. These ranged from eyeglasses to blindness, walkers to wheelchairs, and from hearing aids to total deafness. Seniors may have trouble seeing or hearing the pastor, or even getting into a church building. This often causes alienation.

Secondly, there are emotional barriers. Especially if a person moves into a new community, they find they do not know anyone in the new church. The liturgy is different. They feel out of place. They are alienated. That can happen even if they do not move; new members join the church, old friends die or move away, they are no longer asked to serve on committees, a new pastor is called, and again alienation can set in, and church will just feel different to them and they slowly drop out.

Finally, the clergy also have to share the blame. Too often the pastor has the tragic idea that the senior adult is not too important to his ministry. Or worse, he may see the elderly as a hindrance to ministry. It goes like this; "older members can't help me in ministry. They can't contribute financially to the congregation because of their fixed incomes. Because of their health problems I'm going to be tied down with hospital calls and shut-ins. Why bother?" Someone with that kind of narrow perspective might not actively impede the membership of seniors, but he certainly is not going to work as hard at assimilating the elderly as he would younger persons seeking membership in his congregation.

This type of thinking reflects societal attitudes and standards that conflict with God's expectations. In earlier days, our society regarded the senior as someone to look to for wisdom, knowledge, and leadership. But times have changed. Now when someone reaches age 65, we are ready to discard them as useless. On the part of society, that attitude is irresponsible. On the part of the church, it is inexcusable.

REDUCTION OF ALIENATION

Research strongly indicates that if we wish to increase church attendance among the elderly we first need to find methods to decrease alienation. Two areas that need examination are the physical and emotional barriers to worship.

A. Physical Barriers

As noted earlier, 98 percent of those tested had some type of physical impairment. Here are some suggestions to make worship somewhat easier:

1. *Accommodate wheelchairs.* Have adequate wheelchair ramps, and remove a pew or two in the front of the church. Having space up front for wheelchairs facilitates easy distribution of the Sacrament, as well as makes it easier for the person to see and hear the service. It will also allow the church to keep the narthex clear for any emergencies or easy exiting for members. If pew removal is not feasible, remove the cap-strip on the end of the pew so that when people are sliding into the pew they will not bruise their legs and buttocks. Bathroom facilities also should be accessible to wheelchairs. If a church is involved in a building program, consider keeping everything on one level for easy access.

2. *Accommodate eyesight impairments.* Reserve seating near the front of the sanctuary and equip those pews with sight-saving hymnals and liturgy. Use contrasting colors for walls and floors. Those with depth-perception problems can have a hard time determining where the floor ends and the wall begins. This can cause a person to lose his/her balance and stumble and fall.

3. *Accommodate hearing impairments.* Equip some pews with hearing devices. It is true that many of the elderly have hearing aids, but in a church equipped with an electronic organ, the frequency that the organ emits often causes feedback in the hearing aid, causing a loud squeal in the ear.

4. *Accommodate the incontinent.* Because no one wants to have an "accident" on the carpeting, it helps to carpet the aisles only. Serious thought ought to be given as to whether to purchase padded pews, when one considers the possible embarrassment to a person who may be incontinent.

Something else to consider is the drive-in service. Some churches have placed speakers in the parking lot, so that people can stay in their cars and still worship. Others use local drive-in theaters for that worship experience. Such services can make worship much more comfortable for those with various impairments.

These suggestions may seem expensive or unnecessary, but if one wishes to minister to all of God's kingdom, they may need to be done.

B. *Emotional Barriers*

When discussing the emotional barriers to worship, we first need to be concerned with the concept of bonding. Bonding is the process by which a person attaches to and makes a social connection with another person. Bonding creates a unity that is difficult to eradicate.

Alienation could be described as being "bondless" within a social organization. Let us illustrate by way of example:

About 20 years ago, a family moved from New York to Florida. They claimed to be Presbyterian, but seldom worshiped. They were on the roles of a congregation but not active at all. Ten years later the wife's father retired and also moved to Florida. She began occasionally taking him to church, but over a ten year period they often remarked how they never felt a part of the Florida congregation. At church no one ever spoke to them or was friendly. They were alienated and so they attended only once or possibly twice a year. Two years ago the woman's father died and was buried from that church. Another member happened to see the funeral announcement in the Sunday bulletin and recognized it as a name she knew from her hometown of Bellport, Long Island. The woman called the daughter and asked if she was from Bellport—and she indicated that she was. It turned out that these two women had grown up together, attended the same High School, and their sisters were best friends. The bond was set. The woman became very active in the congregation and still is today. The bond had existed between the two families for years, but in this true example the bond was reestablished in a new social context. The "re-found" friend introduced the woman to others in the congregation and very soon she was an active responsible church member.

Bonding can be a strong influence on the integration of new people, including seniors, into the parish.

Bonding can be facilitated by introducing new people in the church to members originally from the same area of the country. One might use a large pin map to locate the cities of origin of each member of the congregation. Such a procedure helps reestablish bonds in a new social context. The bonds at first may be weak but they will be strengthened in time.

Groups can be formed based on areas of origin, or other similarities of background and interest. Some churches use retired pastors to lead or coordinate such groups for dinners, trips, and Bible Studies. Do not underestimate the love and care people have for their pastor. Start a special Bible Study for seniors only, and have the pastor lead it, the senior will come to cherish that hour or two spent with the pastor. Such activities integrate seniors into the congregation.

At the same time look at seniors as a valuable resource for church work, including calling on the sick, serving on boards, church maintenance and other odd jobs. The senior is blessed with an abundance of time and is very often ready, willing, and able to assist in a variety of ways. An excellent example of that is a program in the Lutheran Church—Missouri Synod called the Laborers for Christ. This is a program in which retired persons use their skills for such projects as helping to construct new churches. The help given by these individuals can greatly reduce the cost of new church construction. The church is greatly benefited and the people are able to contribute in a very meaningful way to the proclamation of the Gospel. Simply, they are using their retirement to the Glory of God in a very special way.

The entire congregation must see the senior member as a responsible, dynamic part of the church. The senior must also see himself in that light. Use the sermon to sensitize the congregation to their role and responsibility to each other as well as the senior. Use the liturgy to help the integration of new members. Especially today, with rapid and often complete liturgical changes being introduced into parishes, it is important to realize that change can alienate. One might delay introduction of the new hymnals if one's parish has many retired persons coming into it. Finally, consider investing in a video cassette recorder to tape worship services for replay in nursing homes, hospitals and for the shut-ins. Why should seniors be forced to "worship" with Schuller, Falwell, Angley, The 700 Club and other sects incompatible with one's own religious background?

It may sound as though special efforts ought to be made to "accommodate" the senior within the church. In reality it is merely suggested that the church should offer the same amount of care to seniors as it would to any other person or group.

When Christ said, "come unto me all ye that are weak and heavy laden," He extended the invitation to all—not just those up to age 65. If we can promote a sense of communion for seniors within the congregation, if we can make them feel a part of that fellowship, the initial obstacles to integration can be overcome. And with that we can truly minister to our senior saints.

REFERENCES

Cox, H. (1978). *Focus: Aging, Annual Editions.* Guilford, CT: Dushkin Publishing.

Huntsberger, D. & Billingsly, P. (1973). *Elements of Statistical Inference.* Boston: Allyn and Bacon.

King, H. (1969, 1967). Dimensions of Religiosity. *Journal for the Scientific Study of Religion.*

McCall, R. (1975). *Fundamental Statistics for Psychology.* New York: Harcourt, Brace and Jovanovich, Inc.

Robinson, M. (1978). *Measures of Social Psychological Attitudes.* Ann Arbor, MI: University of Michigan.

Shaw, W. (1971). *Scales for the Measurement of Attitudes.* New York: McGraw-Hill.

Providing Pastoral Care for the Elderly in Long Term Care Facilities Without a Chaplain Utilizing Coordinated Congregational Resources

Edwin R. Schwanke, B.D.

ABSTRACT. Elderly persons living in long term care facilities are often separated from or have no pastoral care sources. Spiritual care by chaplains was not available in any of the six nursing homes in Wausau, Wisconsin. Twelve Lutheran congregations in the area worked out a plan to provide the necessary pastoral care.

The congregations formed a coordinating agency, Greater Wausau Christian Services, Inc. Through the services of one staff person, the director, who enlisted the lay and pastoral resources of the participating congregations, pastoral care was provided. Worship led by the pastors, meaningful visits made by trained and supervised lay people, and the availability of a trained chaplain became a reality for nearly seven hundred residents in the six long term care facilities.

At one time or another twenty percent of the people over sixty-five spend some time in nursing homes. Many of these long term care facilities do not have a chaplain or established pastoral care plan for their residents. Is there a way to provide quality pastoral care for the growing number of elderly persons who live in nursing homes without a chaplain?

Twelve Lutheran congregations in Wausau, Wisconsin (population 32,000) have found a way to care for the nearly seven hundred residents living in six long term facilities. None of these nursing homes had or continues to have a full-time chaplain.

The congregations carefully surveyed unmet spiritual needs of long term care facility residents. After determining that a significant

Edwin R. Schwanke is Director, Greater Wausau Christian Services. His address is 903 Second Street, Wausau, Wisconsin 54401-4798.

57

number were not receiving pastoral care and that existing pastoral care services needed improvement, the twelve churches decided to act. They formed a nonstock corporation, promised pastoral, lay and financial support, and began the search for a Director. A Lutheran pastor with parish experience and a clinical pastoral education background was called to be the first director of Greater Wausau Christian Services, the name selected for the coordinating agency.

The new director began his work in January, 1981, comparing survey results with first hand visits and conversations with nursing home residents and staff. Three needs headed the list of pastoral care concerns: (1) weekly worship services; (2) meaningful visits with the residents; and (3) the availability of a pastor for the elderly who had none. A number of other concerns were also uncovered: unmet spiritual needs of the residents' families and the nursing home staff, and a frequently mentioned request for Bible study for the residents.

WORSHIP SERVICES

To provide opportunities for worship, pastors of the supporting congregations as well as several other pastors were enlisted to conduct weekly worship services. The director worked with the pastors and conducted workshops on effective worship for the elderly. At the same time he met with nursing home department heads to improve the institutional setting for worship, especially in the two homes without chapels.

VISITS WITH RESIDENTS

Meaningful visits to the elderly long term care facility residents was next priority. Robert N. Butler in *Why Survive? Being Old in America* (1975) wrote "Trained listeners—not necessarily professionals—should be available for the elderly to talk to." Listening was only one of the skills needed for meaningful visits. Others included an understanding of feelings, communication skills, use of Christian resources, grief and loss, depression, death and dying.

The Stephen Series, a lay training series produced by Stephen Ministries was selected as the training instrument. The Series offered background studies in the areas mentioned above and even more regarding the world of shut in elderly persons. The director attended a two week training conference on the Stephen Series in the summer of 1981. When he returned, with the assistance of the twelve sponsoring congregations, sixteen persons were recruited for the first Stephen Series training session which began in September, 1981.

Those enrolled in the Stephen Series training made a two year commitment to this ministry to the elderly. They promised to attend the eighteen weekly training sessions, visit one nursing home resident once a week for approximately one hour, and attend supervision sessions twice a month.

The training consisted of core and elective subjects. Core courses included listening skills, feelings, Christian resources, assertion training, helping visits, confidentiality and termination. Electives were grief and loss, depression, death and dying and ministry to elderly shut in persons.

The nursing home staffs assisted in the selection of residents to be visited. They were informed of the Stephen Series training, the subjects covered, and the commitment of those enrolled. At orientation sessions in the long term care facilities the trainees met staff members, were briefed on the resident to be visited, and then introduced to the resident.

As the supervision phase began in February, 1982, the group trained in the Stephen Series curriculum took the name the Stephen Care Team. Supervision sessions were held every two weeks and provided the individual members of the Stephen Care Team the opportunity to share their joys and their frustrations as they visited their residents. Supervision issues included the sexuality of the elderly, differing understandings of confidentiality in the nursing homes, various forms of depression, the role of God in prolonging life and many others. Supervision also includes inservice training, further exploration of topics uncovered in supervision, Stephen Series subjects not covered in the training, sharing of books regarding helping skills, and presentations by community resource people, the hospital chaplain, the Hospice volunteer director, and a local MD with a special background in depression.

In the summer of 1982, two women who had taken the Stephen Series training were recruited for Stephen Series leaders training, the type of training the director took in 1981. They returned from this training to take an active part in teaching some of the Stephen

Series units. During the summer of 1984, two more received leadership training, increasing the teaching staff to five.

Following the same basic pattern five groups of Stephen Care Team persons have been trained. A sixth group began its training in September, 1984. Sixty five persons have completed their training. They have worked on a one to one basis with over a hundred nursing home residents, and are acclaimed as one of the finest volunteer groups in Wausau.

PASTORAL ASSIGNMENTS

The director has been made available as pastor for nursing home residents who do not have a pastor. He has worked with terminally ill residents, dying residents and their families, and conducted a number of funerals. Referrals are made by the staff who have personally met the director or are aware of his availability. The director also has worked informally with nursing home staff members with a variety of concerns, personal and professional. At the same time he has received counsel and support from residents and staff with his own personal and professional concerns.

ADDITIONAL PROGRAM COMPONENTS

Largely at the request of interested residents, the director has conducted Bible study in five of the six long term care facilities served. These classes have met with varying degrees of success. Residents in an intermediate care setting participate well in bible study conducted twice each month. A class in a skilled care facility struggled with issues of participation and alertness as it met at three in the afternoon, too late in the day for the group.

Using a model developed by a local Lutheran elementary school principal, the director has encouraged another Lutheran school and a number of Sunday Schools and weekday schools to involve their children in ministry to nursing home residents. In preparation for visits to long term care facilities, the children are challenged to wrestle with their own aging, the aging of parents, grandparents and great-grandparents. They are briefed by nursing home personnel who visit them in their classrooms and prepare them for what they will encounter in the nursing home. They prepare a presentation, often a worship service, for the residents. They visit the residents in their rooms, get to know their names before taking them to the planned activity. The children stay with their resident during the service, spend time with them as refreshments are served, and then take them back to their rooms. From visit to visit the children have experienced the illness and death of the resident they had previously visited. This provides a rich opportunity for the young person to grow in awareness and feelings concerning illness and death, and to struggle with the role of God in human life.

PROGRAM STAFF AND FUNDING

The coordinating agency, Greater Wausau Christian Services Inc., providing pastoral care to six Wausau area nursing homes, has one staff person. Depending heavily on the priesthood of all believers, all other work is done by volunteers. The agency has a part time volunteer secretary. Larger mailings are prepared with the assistance of participating congregations. Opportunities for volunteer service are publicized through the twelve congregations.

The director meets monthly with the Board of Directors, composed of a representative from each of the twelve supporting congregations. Together the director and the Board plan and evaluate the agency's ministry which includes pastoral care to the County Jail and the mental health care center. In addition to the Board member, each congregation has a number of Delegates who meet quarterly to consider the work of the agency and who serve as liaison between Greater Christian Services and their congregation.

Greater Wausau Christian Services is funded by the participating congregations, a number of non-member congregations interested in the ministry, and by individuals concerned for this type of pastoral care. Funding by the member congregations is on a per confirmed member basis. The number of confirmed members in the twelve congregations is approximately 11,000, and the per confirmed member share for 1984 is $3.00. Funding began in 1980. Well over ninety percent of funds requested have been received.

One church has provided funding for the past three years even though the congregation is not part of Greater Wausau Christian Services. They are not able at this time to assume full financial responsibility ($3.00 per confirmed member), but are able to provide about $1.00 per confirmed member. The Greater Wausau

Christian Services Board has offered this church a partial membership based on their interest and financial support, and this church has accepted the offer by sending observers to Board meetings. Another church has also begun to fund Greater Wausau Christian Services and will be offered an arrangement similar to the one explained above.

The final funding source is a number of congregations and individuals interested in the ministry. The congregations have no plan to become part of the ministry, but support the pastoral care goals. Several individuals contribute on the same basis.

PROGRAM EVALUATION

Evaluation of the ministry of Greater Wausau Christian Services is done annually by the Board of Directors. The past year of activity is reviewed in preparation for the annual meeting of the delegates in February. Further evaluation of the ministry is done in consultation with nursing home staff. Quarterly, the worship program in each facility is reviewed with the staff person in charge of religious services. The Stephen Care Team ministry is considered in detail at least twice a year as orientation sessions for new Team members are held. These evaluations are done with the long term care facility social workers.

PROGRAM BENEFITS

The pastoral care ministry of Greater Wausau Christian Services is designed to provide supportive Christian services for frail elderly living in long term care facilities. They benefit from the availability of worship services and Bible study, and the opportunity to visit with a caring volunteer. If the resident has no pastor, one is available through Greater Wausau Christian Services. Furthermore, the residents in six nursing homes benefit from the coordinated pastoral care approach. Potentially seven hundred residents could receive services under the direction of one staff person. These are residents in long term care facilities which would hardly consider providing a staff chaplain.

The circle of those who benefit from this ministry widens outward from the nursing home resident to include many others. The pastors of the participating congregations have a much better feeling toward the nursing home as a focus for ministry, and the home as a setting for worship. The pastors are known and recognized as part of the caring team providing a variety of Christian services for the residents. The pastors also feel good that there is an intentional plan for the care of long term care facility residents. Knowing that the plan includes a lay visitation approach, the Stephen Series which involves training and supervision, makes it easier for the pastors to invite lay people to become part of the ministry.

The Stephen Care Team members also benefit through their training and supervision. They are not only trained to help the elderly deal with depression, grief and loss, death and dying, but they personally deal with their own depression, loss and mortality. The training and supervision create a caring community of friends who know how to support one another.

A functioning pastoral care plan is a benefit to the nursing homes served by it. Excellent resident care is a goal of long term care facilities. Resident care is enhanced by opportunities for worship, meaningful visits by trained and supervised volunteers, and the availability of a trained chaplain for extraordinary and emergency pastoral care. Caring nursing home staff people who have little time to spend with the residents, feel better to know they are receiving thoughtful care.

There are financial benefits inherent in the ministry of Greater Wausau Christian Services. As stated before, none of the six facilities served has any chaplaincy staff. None of them have any plans to add this position, stating that financially, it is impossible. Yet quality pastoral care in all the facilities is possible through the congregations' funding of one staff person. The lay and pastoral resources of a dozen congregations have been enlisted through the coordination of one staff person. Certainly, all pastoral care needs cannot be met this way, but it is a very significant step toward comprehensive quality pastoral care for a manageable financial investment.

Finally, the ministry of Greater Wausau Christian Services, providing pastoral care to six nursing homes, channelling the resources of twelve congregations, coordinated by one staff person, provides a model for other communities who see a number of pastoral care opportunities that need attention. These communities are frequently frustrated in their uncoordinated attempts to meet those needs. The Wausau model needs to be considered by other communities which are serious about quality care for elderly persons living in long term care facilities.

REFERENCE

Butler, Robert N. *Why Survive? Being Old in America.* New York: Harper & Row, Publishers, 1975.

Life Care Ministry:
The Church as Part of
the Elderly Support Network

Jean E. Thompson, M.S.W.

ABSTRACT. As St. John's Lutheran Church in Stamford, Connecticut recognized that senior citizens comprised about 18% of its membership, the congregation decided to hire a full-time staff person to develop and direct a ministry program with the elderly. The program offers group meetings, information and referral, direct services, and visitation. It provides spiritual, educational, and fellowship opportunities, and supports the elderly's independence. Instruction about aging, and involvement of younger members in this ministry, has drawn the congregation together with a sense of understanding, community, and mutual responsibility. St. John's approach demonstrates the important role churches can have in the support network of the elderly.

The obligation to be charitable to others is fundamental to the Judeo-Christian tradition. Jewish law says that if an Israelite becomes poor and cannot support himself, his neighbor should provide for him (Leviticus 25:35-37). Jesus later affirms the virtue of charity as he speaks of the final judgement. "Come, you that are blessed by my Father! Come and possess the kingdom . . . I was hungry and you fed me, thirsty and you gave me a drink; I was a stranger and you received me in your homes, naked and you clothed me; I was sick and you took care of me, in prison and you visited me" (Matthew 25:35-36). Throughout history the church has maintained this charitable tradition. The church has been in the forefront of providing care for the poor, the sick, the mentally impaired, the

Jean E. Thompson is Director of Life Care Ministry, St. John's Lutheran Church. Her address is 884 Newfield Avenue, Stamford, Connecticut 06905.

orphans, and the elderly (Reid, 1973). This care has come in the form of hospitals, orphanages, schools for the handicapped, and homes for the aged.

Today, with people living longer and remaining healthier, nursing homes and homes for the aged serve the needs of only 5% of the elderly population. The church must now turn its attention to meeting the needs of the numerous elderly living outside institutions. Most senior citizens are relatively healthy and active. They are seeking meaningful activities for their retirement days. Some desire recreational activities, others are more service oriented. As health deteriorates some assistance may be needed to facilitate a person remaining at home. Mental health, spiritual growth, physical well-being—these are the needs of the elderly which the church must now address.

Churches have a definite responsibility for working with the elderly. The elderly feel that the church and religion are very important. Many claim that religion is the most important influence in their lives. They have a higher attendance rate at church than any other age group and they comprise about 40% of the membership in Christian churches (Moberg, 1983). For the elderly the church is not only a place of worship but also a place to meet old friends, a proponent of a particular way of life, and a source of help in time of need.

St. John's Lutheran Church in Stamford, Connecticut, has acknowledged its responsibility for elderly members through the establishment of a Life Care Ministry Program. This program is designed to nurture and care for older members by engaging them in meaningful activity and sustaining them in their times of need.

DEVELOPMENT OF THE LIFE CARE MINISTRY

In 1963 St. John's Lutheran Church was presented with a gift of $300,000 in stocks. The donors' only request was that the money be used to expand the church's ministry. The congregation agreed, in light of the growing number of older people within society and within the congregation, that the money would be designated for developing a service with seniors. To assure the designated use of the money, an endowment fund was established separate from the church's operating budget.

An exploratory study for an appropriate ministry program first focused on constructing elderly housing. The study group knew that elderly housing existed in the community, usually with supportive services, and always with a waiting list of at least one year. Numerous possibilities were explored for the housing project—cooperative ventures with other churches or the city; various locations; different apartment styles; and additional funding sources. However, cooperative ventures and additional funding did not materialize. Despite an increase in the endowment fund value to $850,000, the fund would only cover construction costs for an apartment complex of 20 units. Since no supportive services (rent subsidies, congregate meals, nursing care) could be offered with the proposed housing, and the number of units was so few, the congregation agreed that construction of elderly housing was not the best ministry choice. The idea of building was abandoned and another exploratory study was begun.

The second study focused on the need for supportive services to help the older members living in the community remain independent. Review of the literature showed that churches across the country provide a wide variety of services for seniors (Clingan, 1975; Cook, 1976). These include advocacy, counseling, day care, education, in-home services, meals, retirement training and transportation. To determine the needs in the local area, interviews were first conducted with area service providers to learn what services already exist for older adults. St. John's study committee found that all basic needs were served to some extent by community agencies, including food, housing, health and transportation. Next, individuals and small groups of St. John's seniors were polled to see how they perceived service and programming needs. Seven needs were commonly mentioned: the need for visitation; escorted transportation; emergency aid; chore service; financial planning; social contacts with other church members; and intergenerational programs. Finally, church leaders were asked their opinions on program structure and design. They urged the study committee to consider expanding the identified service group beyond the elderly, to include adult children of aging parents and others with special needs.

Based on the findings of this exploratory study, the congregation approved a program proposal to develop a Life Care Ministry program, emphasizing the nurture and care of the elderly and others with special needs, through appropriate educational, social and service programs.

DESIGN OF THE LIFE CARE MINISTRY PROGRAM

After the congregation approved the establishment of the Life Care Ministry Program, the study committee developed the following objectives for the program:

a. Establish a senior citizen group with church members.
b. Investigate and utilize community resources and services.
c. Conduct a public relations campaign within the congregation and the community announcing the program, requesting ideas, and inviting referrals.
d. Recruit and train volunteers to assist in providing certain services.
e. Develop a program which addresses the concerns of the families of the elderly.

Although most of these objectives could be met through volunteers, it was recognized that there were many benefits to be gained by hiring a staff person to direct the program. Under the director's administration, the program would be implemented more quickly and also relieve the Pastor of the organizational responsibility. Since St. John's has only one ordained minister, having another staff member would also lend him assistance with members requiring special care. The person hired would give professional direction to the program and recruit and coordinate the volunteers.

St. John's Life Care Ministry Director is part of the church staff in a full-time position (45-50 hours per week) under the administrative authority of both the pastor and a six-member committee elected by the congregation. The committee meets once a month to receive reports from the director, and to give support and guidance for the program. The committee is also responsible for preparation of the annual program budget for approval by the congregation.

The Life Care Ministry, although a program of the church, is supported solely by the interest from its endowment fund. The program does contribute to the operating budget of the church to cover utilities, secretarial services, and office expenses. The first year's budget, including staff expenses, was $34,000. The second year's budget rose by 9% to $37,000, reflecting program expansion as well as inflation. With fewer financial restrictions than the average church budget, the Life Care Ministry is free to be responsive to the needs of the people.

ST. JOHN'S LIFE CARE MINISTRY PROGRAM

The Life Care Ministry Program became a reality in November of 1983. Using the stated objectives as a goal, work began with learning to know the older members of the church. One hundred and ten persons (18% of the congregation) were identified as 65 years of age or older. These people would be the primary (though not exclusive) focus of the Life Care program.

The seniors of St. John's are a very active, mobile and aware group. They can be characterized as relatively healthy (90% are competent in the tasks of daily living); independent (87% live in their own homes); and enjoying an adequate income for their needs and pleasures. Over half (57%) of the seniors are married; 75% drive their own cars. They have an educational level above that of the average older person: most have finished high school, and many are college graduates, several with graduate and postgraduate degrees. Very few could be labeled as frail elderly. Only 2 people are in nursing homes, 4 live in apartments with supportive services, and 8 live with family.

To know how to best develop the details of the Life Care Ministry, the director visited almost every older individual of the church. This initial personal contact was intended to establish rapport with the people, to gain their support and to encourage their participation in the various events. Their input regarding the program was also sought. The program concept was explained and people were invited to add their ideas for programming and services. The visits also afforded a chance to explore individual areas of interest, assess possible or immediate service needs and note volunteer and leadership potential.

Friendly home visits did not cease after the initial gathering of information. They remain an integral part of the ministry. Our goal is to visit each elderly family unit at least twice a year. With most people the contact is much more frequent than that. We visit one woman every week as part of her hospital discharge plan to alleviate depression. Visits help to ease loneliness, maintain contact with the church family, cement bonds of friendship, and keep the church familiar with individual needs. Volunteers have been trained to assist with visiting the shut-ins. Their training dealt with communication techniques, confidentiality, dealing with emotions, recognizing signs of hidden health problems, and practical hints for helping. Currently five women make regular visits to seven individuals. In addition three men are faithful visitors to members in the hospital. People enjoy the volunteers' visits and look forward to their return.

Volunteers help in many ways besides visiting. They provide the supportive services needed by some to remain in the community. Volunteers provide escort and transportation to medical appointments, hair appointments, church services and special events. They also prepare and deliver meals, assist with personal and grocery shopping, and deliver tapes of the Sunday worship service. These are things which would not be available without volunteer assistance.

Volunteers also help with preparations for the seniors' monthly meetings. One day of every month the Bylin Club for Seniors meets for a program or trip, always with a meal included. The Bylin Club, so named in honor of the couple who gave the endowment, is open to all seniors of St. John's. Although many of the seniors are involved in community-sponsored senior organizations, the group meetings provide a fellowship opportunity which many of the seniors desire.

Meeting programs are planned by a six member Advisory Board. The board consists of four senior members, the Life Care Director, and the Pastor. Together they outline the various meeting agendas for six months ahead. During the summer and fall months special trips are planned to local points of interest. These are very popular and have an average attendance of about 30 to 35 people. During the other eight months the programs are of an educational or cultural nature. Health issues are a great concern to the elderly; topics such as exercise and the heart usually have about 20 people attending. People also enjoy speakers on local history and architecture. Issues of taxes and finances are of interest to the group too, but crime prevention and safety have not aroused much interest. The Bylin Club sponsored a big program on J. S. Bach during 1985, celebrating his 300th anniversary. The entire congregation was invited to a covered-dish luncheon after church, followed by a concert with strings, recorders, flute, choir, organ and harpsichord. This was a great success with over 100 people present, more than a third of them seniors.

Average attendance at a Club meeting is between 20 and 30. Some people are very regular in their attendance, while others come only when the topic interests them. Faithful attendance solely for the fellowship takes time to grow. Over half of St. John's seniors have participated in at least one program or trip. Of those seniors who do not participate, 10% are shut-ins, 8% participate in no church activity including worship, and 5% still work full or part time.

The spiritual needs of the older members are of constant concern. Devotions are a part of each meeting. Periodically, meetings are planned on a specific religious topic such as the Holy Land or church efforts for world hunger relief. Special Bible Studies and noon-day services are offered during the Lenten season, and usually have 20 people present. An adult class during Vacation Church School aroused lively discussion among the six who attended and will be offered again. There is desire among some of the seniors to adopt a mission or service project toward which they could contribute of their talents and resources. This would expand the focus of the group beyond themselves while helping others.

Many of the seniors are very service-oriented. They volunteer in organizations such as the Red Cross, Service Corps of Retired Executives (SCORE), local hospitals and museums. Some give many hours of service to the church. The seniors are also very helpful and concerned for each other. They maintain an effective telephone reassurance program and a reliable transportation system. This spirit of helping others is encouraged as the best solution for meeting needs.

With the care between the seniors and the added resource of additional volunteers, many of the needs which arise among the elderly members of St. John's can be met from within the church family. This does not mean that we are striving for self-sufficiency apart from the community. As the exploratory study showed, there are numerous services available through local agencies. When a problem exists which is appropriate for referral to a community agency, the necessary contacts are quickly made. Through the Life Care Ministry Program, St. John's has become a part of the local service network, offering staff time or meeting facilities to community nonprofit groups, senior citizen special events, and city-sponsored continuing education classes. There is also an exchange of information, current happenings, new resources, service needs and ideas occurring regularly within the established network.

A long-term goal of the Life Care Ministry is to expand our focus beyond the congregation into the surrounding community. This is happening in a small way through our representation on the Council of Churches and Synagogues' Task Force on Congregational Outreach to the Elderly. This ecumenical task force is looking for any service gaps existing in the community, and will then attempt to organize the local churches and synagogues to provide the service needed to fill the gap. The services needed may include a nursing home chaplaincy, a caregivers program, or chore service.

Keeping the older people informed of all the church-sponsored activities, community events, and local resources is done through the monthly newsletter published as part of the Life Care program. Each issue contains a feature article on an issue or service. Recent topics include Glaucoma, Wills and Trusts, Heart Disease, Medication Safety, and Hospice. The newsletter also promotes the upcoming monthly meeting or trip, as well as other items of interest. In addition, a bulletin board outside the office of the program director has a regularly changing format of news and information for the seniors. Upcoming events are featured, as is information on issues of health, politics, religion, and local news. Notice of each Bylin Club meeting is also highlighted in the church's weekly bulletin for any newcomers or other interested persons. These also keep the activities of the Life Care Ministry visible to the whole congregation.

As was affirmed in the design of the Life Care Ministry, it is not exclusively for the elderly. This leaves room for programming to serve anyone in need. Most of the problems referred to the Life Care Ministry Program to date have involved an aging concern. Usually these involve working with adult children of aging parents or relatives. Nursing home placement, home care needs, and behavior changes are the most frequently presented problems. A three-part, seven hour seminar designed for children of aging parents was conducted to address some of the common concerns of health, mental health, behavior changes, and resources. About 40 people from both the church and the community attended. Many questions were answered by the doctors, nurses, and social workers as they presented their topics. Participants were also assured they are not alone in their struggles to cope. There is a follow-up session on coping strategies planned for later in the year. Other educational programs planned for the congregation include one on wills and trusts and one on healthy living.

The Life Care Ministry's mandate to provide information to the congregation includes all ages. Youth programs and Sunday School classes have been devoted to topics on aging. Simulation games such as *The End of the Line* (Horn, 1975) and *All About Aging* (Menks, 1984) have been used to promote understanding of, and develop sensitivity for, old age. The youth have learned that old age can bring with it physical limitations which hamper the accomplishment of household chores while the desire to remain in the home is still high. Periodically, the youth are organized to provide chore service to some of the seniors. This usually occurs in the fall during leaf-raking season. The young people enjoy the activity and sense of helping, while the seniors appreciate the assistance.

As plans and programs were developing within the guidelines of the initial objectives, additional needs were identified and additional programs were begun. Cassette tapes of the Sunday worship service are delivered weekly to 3 shut-ins of the St. John's. Tape recorders are available on loan for those who require them. Even if unable to attend the service, those at home can hear the Word of God preached, and join in familiar hymns and liturgy.

We hold an annual Diamond Jubilee to honor our members who are 75 years old and older. A late afternoon dinner with entertainment and special honors ceremony pays tribute to the elders among the older adults.

For anyone experiencing extreme hardship, financial assistance is available through the Life Care program. This is a fund of last resort for financial crises, such as medical needs not covered by insurance. On a day-to-day basis the church maintains a food pantry for anyone needing non-perishable food items.

A Bereavement Program has been newly instituted whereby the minister and Life Care director arrange to visit a bereaved family on a regular basis for a two year period after the death. Helpful information brochures on grief, legal matters, and finances are made available to those adjusting to a loss. Counseling or group support can be arranged on an individual basis.

These programs and services are just the beginning of a vital and growing ministry at St. John's. As people continue to learn of the program and request additional services and programs, the Life Care Ministry will expand in response. The program has experienced encouraging success during the first two years in meeting the given objectives, demonstrating great potential for the future.

The current objectives for the program continue to address the same concerns as did the initial objectives: group meetings, community networking, publicity and information, volunteer services, and aid to families of the aging. Our emphasis has changed from the development phase of these programs to their continuation and growth. To further our service goals, we will seek increased participation, expanded outreach, and additional programs for our members' needs. We hope to continue to respond creatively to identified needs which may arise.

BENEFITS OF THE LIFE CARE MINISTRY PROGRAM

The congregation of St. John's Lutheran Church, by their vote to create a staff position dedicated primarily to the nurture of older members, has declared a concern for older people. The Life Care Ministry has translated that concern into a working program. Older adults at St. John's are a visible and viable component of the church's life. The elderly are feeling positive about themselves and enjoy the personal attention by a member of the church staff. Others in the congregation are beginning to be aware of the seniors as an active, talented, intelligent and caring group of people. Intergenerational programs are very successful. The Bach luncheon and concert previously described is an example.

Seniors are beginning to look forward to their meetings each month. Some not yet of senior age are anticipating their eligibility. Several older people are renewing their worship life due to their involvement with the Life Care program. They are confident of knowing someone at church on Sunday mornings, rides are arranged for them, and special service helps are available.

The Life Care program serves as an advocate for the seniors of St. John's. Senior concerns are brought before the Church Council each month now whereas previously there was no one to raise the issues. Awareness is the main goal of the advocacy, although occassionally there is a call to action. One such instance involved the modification of the restrooms for easier access and improved safety.

Everyone benefits from the Life Care Ministry. Seminars promote understanding of aging, both of others and of self. Special equipment such as a proposed barrier-free ramp into the sanctuary would benefit the younger arthritic as well as the old. Large print service books, library materials, and devotional aids are helpful for anyone with visual impairments. Programs and personal contacts create new friendships and develop a sense of caring and responsibility for one another. Youth and adults learn, from the seniors' living example, the qualities of patience, courage, faith, and love. They also hear history of near and far as seniors recount their younger days. As a result of coming to know individuals rather than stereotypes, ageism and fear are declining.

Community service agencies and local churches are coming to recognize St. John's as a leader in elderly ministry as a result of the Life Care program. Churches look to St. John's for guidance in developing their own ministry programs among the elderly. The Life Care Director has done training for several churches, teaching volunteers how to make visits to people at home or in the hospital. Word of St. John's Life Care Ministry continues to be spread as more and more people become involved with the various aspects of the program.

CONCLUSION

People 65 years of age and over are a significant force in American society. They constitute 11.3% of the population today, and each year their numbers increase. They are the fastest growing group in America (Butler, 1975). The United States is no longer a youthful nation; it is a graying society.

The population explosion of elderly people has forced changes in our way of thinking and has altered the distribution of social services. Churches also need to recognize and adapt their thinking for the increasing number of older adults. The elderly comprise 30 to 50 percent of the membership in most churches. They often outnumber the youth.

Churches have a responsibility to serve older people just as they have a responsibility to educate the young. Churches are to be concerned with the mental and physical needs of people, as well as their spiritual needs. Programs such as the Life Care Ministry at St. John's strive to provide that kind of total care for the elderly of the congregation.

Although St. John's is exceptional in having an endowment to fund its senior service, the program's framework is still valid as a model for others. The procedure used for developing the Life Care Ministry is:

a. Determine the specific needs of the target population.
b. Recruit people who are committed to this area of ministry and willing to work.

   c. Publicize ideas and implement one or two of the simpler services or programs.

   d. Continue publicity and make personal contacts to involve others.

   e. Expand the program as more people become involved, and continue publicity and personal contacts.

The cycle continues and the program grows as more and more people, both old and young, become involved. This model is applicable for any congregation, large or small, wealthy or not; the key is the desire to help.

REFERENCES

Butler, Robert N., *Why Survive? Being Old in America.* New York, Harper & Row, Publishers, 1975.

Clingan, Donald F. *Aging Persons in the Community of Faith.* Indianapolis: The Indiana Commission on the Aging and Aged, 1975.

Cook, T.C., Jr. *The Religious Sector Explores Its Mission in Aging.* Athens, GA: National Interfaith Coalition on Aging, 1976.

Horn, Ansell T. *The End of the Line.* Ann Arbor, MI: The University of Michigan—The Institute of Gerontology, 1975.

Menks, Ferol A. *All About Aging.* Pacific Palisades, CA: Nurseco, Inc., 1984.

Moberg, David O. The Ecological Fallacy: Concerns for Program Planners. *Generations,* 1983, *8* (1), 12-14.

Reid, William J. Sectarian Agencies. *Encyclopedia of Social Work* (Vol. 2). Washington, D.C.: National Association of Social Workers, 1973.

"Involving the Elderly in Mission"—A Service Project

Patricia C. Breien, M.A.

ABSTRACT. As one church grew from a small immigrant church to a conglomerate of 1,200 members, the natural social networks were no longer adequate to support the population of older persons. Networks had to be made intentional through programming. A needs assessment of the senior population identified specific subgroups and their needs. Recognizing the diversity of the senior population, a broad spectrum of programs was established. An effort was made to maintain a balance between traditional and innovative.

The senior program has strengthened the networking among seniors, increased their integration with the other age groups in the church, and provided an entry level for those new to the church. The program has also become known in the community, which has resulted in cooperation with other senior service organizations who provide education and training. The Area Agency on Aging, realizing the importance of the church to the senior population, has selected a member of the church community to serve on its Advisory Board.

A nine year old friend, Eric, has observed that old people "spend their days sleeping, talking to themselves, and having surgery." Eric is not atypical. At nine he has already been enculturated with an ageist attitude. One can laugh at the candid remarks of a child. It is not humorous when older people themselves have internalized these negative attitudes and see themselves as useless, burdensome, and impaired. Neither Madison Avenue nor the media will attempt to change this image until it is economically profitable. The church in its role as a countercultural agent, must try. In the words of Maggie Kuhn, "Churches and synagogues are going to have to be engaged in a mighty ethical and moral confrontation with the prevailing values of our society" (Kuhn, 1980).

Patricia C. Breien, former Director of Volunteers, Our Savior's Lutheran Church, Greeley, Colorado. Her address is 634-38 Avenue, Greeley, Colorado 80634.

Our Savior's Lutheran Church in Greeley, Colorado was founded as an immigrant church. The congregation was comprised primarily of German-Russian families who lost farms on the Volga during the Russian Revolution. They came to Colorado to work the sugar beet fields. They were strong people, industrious, and they had strong natural social networks.

Today, 50+ years later, the congregation has grown to a conglomerate of 1,200 members with diverse cultural backgrounds. Social and familial networks have weakened. The congregation includes a number of older persons who moved to Colorado after retirement to be near children. These persons have not readily been accepted by the German-Russian core. The pastors have found it more and more difficult, and unwise, to minister to the needs of the growing senior population on an individual basis. It was decided that social and support networks would have to be made intentional through programming. The elderly would be involved in mission to meet the needs of their peers, the congregation, and the community.

PROGRAM DEVELOPMENT

Phase I—GOALS: The "Involving the Elderly in Mission" program was initiated in 1981 by a local Lutheran pastor. The author was doing graduate work in gerontology at that time and was asked to work with the staff and volunteers to coordinate the program. Considerable time was spent in discussion and review of literature to ensure a sound foundation. It was decided that the program's goals would be those of the Life Enrichment for the Elderly Action/ Research Project (Lutheran Brotherhood, 1978), with slight modifications, to develop a program with the elderly within the microcosm of the congregation which would:

1. Provide roles for the elderly which utilize their resources to meet their needs, as well as the needs of the congregation and community.
2. To enhance a sense of self-worth and identity in the elderly.
3. To facilitate the involvement of elderly in action programs on behalf of older persons.
4. To sensitize persons of all ages to the resources and concerns of the elderly.
5. To encourage intergenerational respect and communication.

Phase II—NEEDS ASSESSMENT: After the goals had been agreed upon, but before any specific objectives were drawn up, a needs assessment was done. Members of the senior population of the congregation were randomly selected and asked to participate in group interviews. As a result of these interviews, subgroups within the senior population were identified as having specific needs (See Table I—Identified Needs of the Senior Members of the Church).

Phase III—SENIOR TASK FORCE: Armed with ideas from the needs assessment, from the literature and from the heads of caring, creative people, a list of twenty possible objectives was drawn up. At this stage it was essential that the seniors themselves be involved in and responsible for the program. Therefore, a "Task Force on Aging" was established. The task force consisted of five persons ranging in age from 60 to 75, and the coordinator. Members were carefully chosen for their qualities of leadership and integrity. It was the responsibility of the task force to select and prioritize objectives, to give creative input and direction to the program, and to evaluate the progress of the program. The following were chosen by the task force as initial objectives:

1. To publish a senior directory (large print).
2. To make a color-coded map of senior members classifying each as to level of mobility (drives self, can drive others, needs transportation, shut-in, etc.)
3. To contact other churches and community agencies to determine what services were available.
4. To publish a monthly senior newsletter with information on
   —community services
   —community cultural affairs
   —birthdays, anniversaries
   —special interest radio and TV programs
   —book reviews
   —etc.
5. To form a "senior" choir which would sing from the old hymnals.
6. To hold regular potluck dinners featuring speakers on topics of current interest (not just entertainment).
7. To form groups of seniors interested in golf, tennis, walking, etc.
8. To set up a senior communication board (bulletin board) with information on current legislation affecting seniors, poetry, photography, etc. (for the enlightenment of all ages).

Table I - Identified Needs of the Senior Members of the
Church.

General Needs	Senior Population	Special Needs
Transportation	New widows	Grief support support reintegration handyman skills
Sense of community	New widowers	Grief support support reintegration housekeeping skills
Information and referral services	Shut-ins	Contact
Meaningful roles	Those caring for shut-ins	Time-off support
	New to community	Integration
	Newly retired	???
	Others	Education Social events

Senior volunteers were called and asked to assist with or be responsible for each of the above projects. A former newspaper reporter became editor of the newsletter. A retired teacher wrote book reviews. A retired professor asked MADD (Mother's Against Drunk Drivers) to speak at the first potluck.

OUTSTANDING PROGRAM ELEMENTS

We live in a world in which people are more concerned with cure than with care . . . To care is to be present to those who suffer and to stay present even when nothing can be done to change their situation. To care is to be compassionate and so to form a community of people honestly facing the painful reality of our finite existence. (Nouwen, 1981)

Two of the most successful senior program elements at Our Savior's were "Senior to Senior" and the senior communion service. "Senior to Senior" was started as a response to an overwhelming need for care, contact, and support by seniors in crisis. Caring seniors were asked to volunteer for a period of three months or more. They were to make contact with one or more shut-ins or seniors in crisis, on a weekly basis. The contact was made by telephone, letter, or personal visit. The volunteers went through a training session, and were assigned persons to visit. The volunteers met each Tuesday morning to discuss the needs of those visited, and began to bring some of those visited with them. Refreshments were added, and a short devotion.

The idea of a monthly communion service grew from these meetings. A special effort, including a telephone campaign, was made to get as many shut-ins and less mobile seniors as possible to the communion services. At each communion service, chairs were arranged in a circle formation in the chapel to facilitate eye contact and communication. Each person was communed at his or her own seat so those with ambulatory problems were not embarrassed. Whereas Sunday morning services were large and often hectic, these services were intimate and unhurried. Even those with reduced sight and hearing could follow. Those present were strengthened by word, sacrament, fellowship, and a renewed sense of community.

INTERGENERATIONAL ELEMENTS

The program as described thus far has been age-segregated, i.e. by seniors for seniors. However, as one goal of the program was to encourage "intergenerational respect and communication," age-integrated programming was needed. It was known that in a rapidly changing society the old and young were separated by more than years. They were also separated by culture, value systems, belief systems, etc. But there were constants e.g., playing, learning and death, that crossed all barriers.

One of the more innovative and successful intergenerational programs at Our Savior's has been the bereavement team. Too often when a death was announced in church, the congregation hardly recognized the family's name, much less surrounded and supported that family. A grieving family, hurt by the lack of response, withdrew, and social networks were weakened even further. The bereavement team was formed of six persons, ages 25 to 75, who had experienced death first hand and successfully gone through the grieving process. The role of the group was to give physical and emotional support to anyone in the congregation who had lost a family member or loved one. This support ranged from a sympathy card acknowledging the death, to mobilizing the congregation to provide meals, transportation, and visits long after the funeral was over.

The annual church Halloween Party was another programmed intergenerational event. Each year seniors were asked to serve as costume judges, to man the cake walk, and to help with games. Laughing and playing together has formed bonds. Vacation Bible School has also proved an excellent setting in which to unite young and old. Seniors have taught bread baking, ground flour, made soap, and acted in skits. Both children and seniors grew in the process.

COMMUNITY SERVICES

It was a plus for the seniors of the church that the city abounded in resources for seniors: an active senior center, RSVP, Elderhostel, a peer counseling program, Eldergarten, community college, handicapped transport, etc. As in any area where many services were available, there was some duplication of services and resulting turf protection. Rather than competing with these services, an attempt was made to map them, use them, and invite them into the church facility. The community college was invited to hold classes for city seniors in the church building. Patient Advocacy Team—an organization which provided visitors to nursing home patients—brought nursing home residents to the church once each month to bake cookies. Senior members of Our Savior's planned, cooked and served a weekly interdenominational noon luncheon for 200+ seniors through the auspices of RSVP, for eight years. The Area Agency on Aging held a four day training program for 60 senior volunteers in the church facility. These volunteers were trained to work with elderly on evaluating their Medigap insurance policies.

Not only has this use of church facilities by the community promoted good will, it has also brought excellent services into the church, and helped our seniors with their ministry. Many who were too timid to walk into the RSVP office and ask for a volunteer job, volunteered to help with a project being held in their own church. Success in one experience gave courage to move out to others.

The Area Agency on Aging (AAA), located in the city, has also realized the important role of the church in the lives of elderly persons. The coordinator of Our Savior's program was recently made a member of the AAA advisory board. The board has functioned to monitor local senior service agencies, set policy, and review funding of senior programs. This appointment gave the religious community a voice in policy making decisions i.e., a chance to affect more lives on a broader scale.

REFLECTIONS

The development of Our Savior's senior program has not been a smooth ride. Programs which were thought to be "sure fire" and which generated tremendous excitement among the staff have failed grandly. A "senior" choir never got off the ground. A plan to send a senior to be trained in peer counseling techniques by a geriatric counselor also failed. Hours were spent interviewing and looking for the right person, but no one would go. Lack of leadership has been a problem. There were so many seniors willing to help, and so few willing to lead. Our sense of time had to be changed. Developing and selling ideas took time, and repetition, and more time. Time to listen had to be included in each day's schedule. We struggled with the inclination to "do for," to patronize, to paternalize, and to remove problems rather than support someone in finding his or her own solution.

In spite of all this, we became more and more convinced that the church was an excellent base for senior programs. The facilities were already present, the elderly population was known, registered and fairly homogeneous. Older persons knew churches and what to expect in them. The church was an intergenerational institution, one of the few left, and provided possibilities for intergenerational experiences. In addition, the church had the depth, the theology, to move far beyond other community organizations. The priesthood of all believers, a central tenet of Lutheran theology, does not state that persons retire from this priesthood at 65. The church can provide meaningful roles and purpose for every older person. It can provide community, and the fellowship of believers.

RECOMMENDATIONS TO CONGREGATIONS CONTEMPLATING A SENIOR MINISTRY PROGRAM

There is no formula to ensure a successful program, but much can be done during the planning stages to make a program robust. For example:

1. Include representatives of the senior population in all phases of the planning process. Their knowledge and ideas are essential. Participation will ensure their ownership of the program. And their support will be invaluable when the program idea is to be sold to the other seniors in the congregation.
2. Know community resources. Do not compete with sound, existing programs. Invite them into the church as teachers, support them with volunteers, and develop programs in areas where community resources are lacking.
3. The senior population of any congregation is diverse in age, life experiences, and resources. One simple program cannot serve all of them. Plan a diverse program if energy and resources are available. Otherwise, start with a simple, well defined program and let it develop.
4. Do not be afraid to use persons from other age groups in planning and implementing a senior ministry program. Persons with enthusiasm, leadership skills, sensitivity, or special knowledge are invaluable, no matter what age group they

represent. Do not allow these persons to dominate, but to serve as catalysts to the program.

5. Experiences at Our Savior's have shown that the senior ministry program functions at its peak when the following factors are in balance: ministry, education, fellowship.
6. Beware the natural inclination of many persons to "do for" or to entertain the elderly. The elderly have a ministry. Hold each one accountable to carry it out, according to his or her resources. Help each to experience the joy of caring.
7. As a congregation, recognize the ministry and service of the elderly. Recognize that which is done within the framework of the program and that which is done in the community, as a neighbor and as a friend. It is pleasant to be recognized. It is inspiring to hear what caring persons have done.

Henri Nouwen states that we carry within us a deep-seated resistance against care. Caring means we have to come in touch with our own sufferings, pains and anxieties (Nouwen, 1981). The senior center may opt to exclude minorities, stroke victims, etc., but the church cannot. The church is called to lead its people in the ministry of caring. And the great mystery of caring is that it always involves the healing not only of the one who is cared for, but also of the one who cares (Nouwen, 1981).

REFERENCES

Kuhn, Margaret S. "Spiritual Well-Being As A Celebration of Wholeness." *Spiritual Well-Being of the Elderly*, J.A. Thorson & T.C. Cook, Eds. Charles C. Thomas-Publisher, Springfield, Ill. 1980.

Thompson, G.S. *Life Enrichment for the Elderly*, Lutheran Brotherhood, Minneapolis, MN, 1980.

Nouwen, Henri J.J. "Care And The Elderly." *Aging and The Human Spirit*, LeFevre, & LeFevre, Eds. Exploration Press, Chicago, Ill. 1981.

Educational Opportunities
for Older Adults

Omar G. Otterness, Ph.D.

ABSTRACT. This paper challenges congregations to become centers for life-long learning. An experiment in educational programming conducted by Saint Olaf College at residences of the Ebenezer Society in Minneapolis, Minnesota is reported upon. The benefits derived from the program included: (1) growth in understanding of the Christian faith; (2) better understanding of political issues; (3) greater appreciation of the liberal arts; and (4) personal satisfaction. Also explored are the implications of the experiment for the educational programs of congregations. The greater interest in education by the new generation of elderly presents new opportunities to the churches.

INTRODUCTION

An ancient Chinese proverb says, "If one lives until old and studies continuously, there still remains a large fraction of learning unacquired." In this age of the knowledge explosion when information is said to double every 15 years, the unacquired fraction is larger than ever. To be informed about what is happening in this changing world is a tremendous challenge to older adults.

It is the thesis of this paper that congregations can help meet this challenge by becoming a center for lifelong learning. To support this thesis the author will report on an experiment in providing educational opportunities for older adults, and then draw some implications from it for educational programs in the congregation.

Omar G. Otterness, Route 5, Northfield, Minnesota 55057, is Associate Director of Church Relations, Ebenezer Society.

EXPERIMENT IN EDUCATION PROGRAMS
FOR OLDER ADULTS

The experiment was carried out as a part of the author's sabbatical work in the school year of 1979-80. The setting was the three independent living residences and three supportive living facilities managed by the Ebenezer Society of Minneapolis, Minnesota. It did not take long to realize through daily contact with the residents that there was a hunger for knowledge that had little opportunity to be satisfied. One resident reported that his greatest need was for some source of intellectual stimulation.

In response to this need, a cooperative program between the Ebenezer Society and Saint Olaf College was developed to bring lectures, concerts, and courses to the residents. The model for the experiment came from the successful Elderhostel programs which bring older adults to college campuses. The phenomenal growth of Elderhostel programs on 700 campuses demonstrates the interest in education on the part of a growing number of older adults. The purpose of the experiment at hand was to bring such educational opportunities to the older adults at their places of residence.

Central to the planning was the recognition that older adults must be in charge of their own learning. Thus committees were formed in each of the residences. The average age of one committee was over eighty with the chairperson being over ninety. The committees drew up lists of twenty possible topics for courses and surveyed all residents to determine areas of interest. The lists included offerings in the fine arts, history, languages, literature, music, political science, religion, science, and writing. From the results of this survey, the ten most popular topics were listed on a second survey form and residents were asked to indicate the three topics of most interest to them. The results of this survey determined the courses to be offered during the year.

There were thirty-six events sponsored or coordinated through the project. These involved 104 separate sessions in the various facilities. There were nine short courses and three workshops for which tuition was charged. These more formal educational programs had 286 registrants. There were nine lecture series, fourteen concerts, and other activities for which there was no charge or formal registration. A conservative estimate of attendance for these events would be approximately 3,000 people.

The total expenditure for the program was $6,248. Of this amount, $3,748 was contributed by the residents through tuitions or residential councils. There was also a grant of $500 from the Minnesota Humanities Commission to support one of the courses. The balance of the cost was met by a grant of $2,000 from Saint Olaf College.

In addition to the above, the University of Minnesota World Affairs Center provided lecturers for the Great Decisions series. The Ebenezer Society provided without charge the secretarial and accounting services required by the program.

In the independent living residences, participants were requested to pay ten dollars for each five session course. In the supportive living facilities, there was no charge for the courses. The instructors from Saint Olaf College were paid sixty dollars for each ninety minute session.

The wide range of interests is indicated by the following course and lecture titles:

— Residence 1: Five Women of Faith, American Short Stories, Climbing the Family Tree, Music Appreciation, American Art.
— Residence 2: Images of the Presidency, Scandinavian Civilization, Great Issues of Faith, Great Decisions.
— Residence 3: Greek Civilization, Great Issues of Faith, Climbing the Family Tree, Autobiographical Writing, Scandinavian Civilization, Meaning for the Second Half of Life.
— Supportive Living Residence 1: Scandinavian Immigration, Great Decisions.
— Supportive Living Residence 2: American Musical Theatre, Great Decisions, Norwegian Folk Music and Dance.
— Supportive Living Residence 3: Great Decisions, Scandinavian Immigration.

The program is now commencing its fifth year in the independent living residences. The Ebenezer Society has continued to provide a part-time staff member to facilitate the program, but the income from the tuition has supported the instructional program without assistance from outside grants. It has not been found possible to continue the program in supportive living facilities where tuition could not be charged.

MEANING FOR THE SECOND HALF OF LIFE

It is not possible to describe in detail each of the courses, but it is helpful to report on one course which required greater involvement of the participants. It was different from the other courses in its format. Entitled "Meaning for the Second Half of Life," it was modeled after a program developed by Dr. Ross Snyder of the San Francisco Theological Seminary. Each of the participants wrote brief descriptions of significant experiences in his or her life. The four suggested topics were as follows:

1. A Lived Moment: The account of a moment that made a deep impression on one, such as the first day on the job, the meeting with an important person in one's life, a childhood experience burned into one's memory, etc.
2. A Time of Importance: An account of a length of living, not just a single moment. It could be a period of time which had an impact on one's life. Examples: depression days, war years, crisis times of life, etc.
3. A Personal Manifesto: An account of a time in one's life when one took a stand on an issue or had to make an important decision—"Once I stood up. I was an integrity that had to be taken account of."
4. Saga: Not an autobiography, but an account of significant occasions that helped inform the meanings that give purpose to one's life.

The unique aspect of this life review exercise was the sharing of these life stories in groups of five or six. Each member read her or his account and all the others responded with questions and observations which served to clarify and affirm the meaning of the experience.

The participants appreciated the program as a way to start writing about some of the meaningful experiences of their lives which they could then share with children and grandchildren. It also resulted in a deeper level of friendship and fellowship among the participants.

Although it was not publicized as a religious or spiritual exercise, it became that for many of the participants. One participant summarized the meaning that was clarified for her in these words: "The sense of God's guidance in my life, in both hard and good times, became clear. I can see this now as I look back and find meaning in events that had not seemed so important at the time."

FOUR BENEFITS

It is appropriate to ask what benefits resulted from the total program. There are four that stand out as most important.

Benefit #1

If such a program has as one of its main components the study of the Christian faith, it can contribute to a greater spiritual vitality. At a recent conference, Dr. James Birren, Executive Director of the Andrus Gerontological Center, listed all the different needs of the elderly which the congregation could help meet—fellowship, daycare, meals, etc. (1984). He then suggested that all of these needs could be met by other agencies, but the one primary need for a sustaining meaning and purpose in life could only be fully met by the church. This should be the church's primary concern.

It is often presupposed that older people are more religious and that it is easier to have faith when you are older. There is evidence, however, which suggests that when the outer forms of religious practice have been kept alive primarily by social expectations, even those observances may diminish in later life if there has not been a deepening of personal faith.

James Fowler (1981) has made a study of stages of faith in adult development and related them to the life-cycle theory of Erik Erikson. According to Erikson (1982), the last stage of life requires a higher level of wisdom if integrity is to be maintained over against the temptations to despair. Fowler maintains that faith does not automatically mature with the chronological stages of the life cycle. When faith has been stunted at an immature level, there will not be the inner resources to cope with the challenges of old age.

Participants in the program reported that the insights gained from the fresh study of the faith provided a basis for their reaffirmation of the meaning and purposes of life.

Benefit #2

A second benefit resulting from the program was the opportunity for participants to become better informed citizens. There was great interest in both national and international political issues as presented in the Great Decisions courses. The recognition that political and social responsibility are important aspects of Christian discipleship makes such courses appropriate for sponsorship by con-gregations.

Benefit #3

Through the broad study of the liberal arts there is greater ap-preciation of God's creation. The program emphasized the joy of learning for the sake of learning—the joys of study and new discov-ery. When Paul Tournier (1972) was advised upon retirement to turn away from the world to more spiritual concerns, he replied: "It is because of God that I am interested in the world, because he made it, and put me in it. I do not see why I should be any less interested in it now than when I was young." Searching for more knowledge about God's creation is to love God with the mind.

Benefit #4

There were many benefits that came to individuals which were not directly related to the church or religious faith. One participant reported that her friends had noted a new smile on her face and a brighter gleam in her eye. Psychologist Richard Restak (1979) reports that older adults who are involved in active mental pursuits also enjoy greater physical health. But even when physical health declines, the life of the mind can flourish. One participant in an adult educational program explained his commitment to lifelong learning this way: "If the time comes that I am in some way con-fined, when I cannot run around in person, I will be able to get around in my mind."

PROBLEMS AND CHALLENGES

It is also important to recognize the problems and challenges which emerged in the course of the program. The following issues require further reflection and experimentation.

1. The formal short courses reached only a small percentage of the thousand residents in the three independent living residences. Although there were a total of 286 paid registrations for the nine courses with an average of over thirty per course, many of that number were repeat registrations and thus the total of different par-ticipants was small. There are many elderly with little formal educa-

tion who are afraid of the more structured educational programs. Thus various ways must be sought to overcome this fear. It may help to promote educational programs as fairs, festivals and integrate them with more informal gatherings.

2. The way to reach residents of the supportive living facilities with educational programs presents special problems. In the intermediate care unit, there was a very positive response which indicated that there were many who wanted intellectual stimulation. There was also a minority of residents in the intensive care units who welcomed such opportunities. It is mistaken to presuppose that because there is physical disability there is corresponding mental disability.

Although the offerings were limited, there was a positive response and many individuals found it a rewarding experience. However, there were significant problems. There was often the failure of the instructor to adapt the presentation to the needs of the audience. It requires teachers with great sensitivity and special abilities to reach this audience. Another difficulty was in finding adequate funding to continue the program. Almost half of the Saint Olaf grant was used to subsidize this program because it was not feasible to charge tuition.

The challenge to find ways of meeting these problems remain. It is important because the residents of these facilities have few opportunities for this kind of intellectual challenge. New ways must be explored for meeting the needs of these residents.

IMPLICATIONS FOR CONGREGATIONS

Although limited in scope, it is my conviction that this experiment can serve not only as a model for creative relationships between church colleges and the retirement community but also as a challenge for congregations to develop a fuller educational ministry to and with adults.

It may be unfair to generalize but there is probably a measure of truth in the charge that the church has not given enough attention to adult education. It has been content to let systematic instruction end with youth. There are now developing encouraging exceptions to this charge. However, the present generation of older adults have not had the benefit of this.

When one surveys most congregational activities planned especially for older adults, it is discovered that their primary goals are fellowship, entertainment and touring. While these goals are appropriate, it is important for the church to have more to offer than shuffleboard and coffee. It may be too cynical but Maggie Kuhn (1977) describes most church programs for the elderly as a return to the play pen. Another critic has said that whereas Jesus played with children and taught adults, all too often the church plays with adults and teaches children.

It is my conviction that there are resources in every community to make the congregation a center for lifelong learning. Educators, the retired people themselves, professional people and the clergy are but a few of the resources for leadership.

The importance of preparing to meet this challenge becomes apparent when one observes the changing nature of the older generation. Dr. Bernice Neugarten (1975) reports that not only is there a shift to a larger number of older people in our population, but the new generation of the elderly will have very different education experiences. Today the average city dweller over 65 has had not more than an eighth grade education. Those now in the 45-54 age bracket have an average of over twelve years of education. In 1982, 71% of the population over 25 years of age had completed high school and 18% had graduated from college. A college graduate is almost five times as likely to participate in some form of organized instruction than a high-school dropout. This is not to suggest that only those with more formal education are able to benefit from continuing education, but it does indicate that in the future there will be greater interest in educational opportunities.

CONCLUDING OBSERVATIONS

In conclusion, it remains to state some of the principles that must guide the congregation's program of adult education.

1. As previously stated, adults must be in charge of their own learning. They know what is of interest to themselves. They are the first to perceive what plays down to them. When programs have been devised without their involvement in the planning, they have failed.

2. The presentation of the programs must be sensitive to the feelings of the older person. Some are even too shy to walk into a classroom. Many fear being found wrong before their peers. Too

much adult education deals only with the way people think and does not take into account the feelings and unresolved tensions in many adult lives. Thus such programs must be non-threatening and help the elderly to discern their many gifts.

3. Although the focus of this paper has been on older adults, it is important to realize that such educational programs could be inclusive of all adults. Perhaps they should not be given the label of programs for the elderly because of the hesitancy of many older adults to associate with such programs. As adult education, the courses could bring together the different generations in a common learning experience.

"THE GLORY OF THE LIGHTED MIND"

A reknowned poet once wrote of the "glory of the lighted mind" which sees all of life in the light of Jesus Christ. A program of lifelong learning carried out in the light of Gospel would help to make that a reality. It would bear witness that we have a Christ for all seasons of life—one who calls us to celebrate aging by growing in mind and spirit.

REFERENCES

Birren, J. Aging as a Scientific and Value-laden Field of Inquiry. Paper presented at the National Symposium of The Role of the Church and Aging, Zion, Illinois, September, 1984.

Erikson, E. H. *The Life Cycle Completed.* New York: W.W. Norton, 1982.

Fowler, J.W. *Stages of Faith.* San Francisco: Harper & Row, 1981.

Kuhn, M. E. *Maggie Kuhn on Aging.* Philadelphia: Westminister, 1977.

Neugarten, B. L. "The Future and the Young-Old." *Gerontologist,* Vol. 15:1, February, 1975.

Restak, R. M., *The Brain-The Last Frontier.* New York: Doubleday, 1979.

Tournier, P. *Learn to Grow Old.* San Francisco: Harper & Row, 1972.

Pre-Retirement Planning on the Campus: A New Service for Lutheran Colleges

James H. Shaffer, Ph.D.

ABSTRACT. Fourteen subjects, approximately 50-60 years of age, participated in a six-session, pre-retirement planning workshop held on the campus of Thiel College. Topics covered during the two-hour, weekly sessions were attitudes toward aging and retirement; financial planning; desirable retirement locations; use of leisure time, hobbies and skills; holistic health; and legal affairs. Information on these topics was obtained through large and small group discussions, resource speakers, and homework assignments. Participants gave high evaluations to most aspects of the workshop. It was concluded that Lutheran college campuses can be good sites for pre-retirement planning workshops and that these workshops can be beneficial to the colleges as well as to the participants. Comparison of this workshop with similar ones and modifications of the workshop are also discussed.

INTRODUCTION

Retirement occurs when " . . . a person (1) withdraws fully or partially from the labor force and (2) begins collecting a pension, Social Security benefits, or other retirement income" (McConnell, 1983, p. 394). Inherent in the retirement process are many sources of potential dissatisfaction, such as loss of social roles and status, decrease in income, increased awareness of the aging process, greater likelihood for declining health, and the availability of too much leisure time (Darnley, 1975; Hochschild, 1973; Thurnher, 1974). Despite these potential dissatisfactions, many people seem to enjoy retirement. The literature suggests that positive attitudes toward retirement are most likely to develop under the following conditions: (1) retirement is voluntary; (2) income and health are good enough to live adequately; (3) work is not the most important

James H. Shaffer is Professor of Psychology, Thiel College, Greenville, Pennsylvania 16125.

97

activity in one's life; and (4) some preparation and planning for retirement have occurred (McConnell, 1983).

If pre-retirement planning has been important in the past, demographic trends indicate it will be equally important, if not more important, in the future. Men will likely continue opting for retirement before the age of 65, and the percentage of elderly is predicted to grow from its present value of 11.1% to 12.2% in the year 2000 and 15.5% in the year 2020 (McConnell, 1983; Siegel, 1979). In addition, recent economic uncertainties, such as fluctuating inflation rates and instability in the Social Security and Medicare systems, should increase the motivation for sound pre-retirement planning.

Many people, if left to their own devices, do not have either the motivation or the knowledge to plan adequately for retirement. Pre-retirement workshops, however, provide a structure for exchanging attitudes and concerns about retirement with peers and for acquiring more detailed information through homework assignments and resource speakers (e.g., investment planners, Social Security representatives, dieticians, lawyers, etc.) While content varies, most workshops include some, if not all, of the following topics: attitudes toward retirement, financial planning, leisure time activities, health maintenance, housing needs, and legal affairs.

Several events led the author to offer "So You Want a Good Retirement." A needs analysis conducted among the constituents of the college (e.g., alumni, synod clergy, local businessmen, and townspeople) indicated a demand existed for such a workshop. In addition, the author and his wife are trained pre-retirement workshop leaders, and had previously conducted two SMART workshops on campus. SMART (Senior Member and Retiree Training) was designed by the Aid Association for Lutherans as a service to be offered through the Association's local branch organizations. The remainder of this paper discusses the planning, implementation, and evaluation of the author's own workshop "So You Want a Good Retirement."

METHOD

Subjects

Subjects for this workshop included six couples and two unrelated individuals, all 50-60 years of age. At least one member of each couple and both unrelated individuals were employed. All lived within a 30-mile radius of Thiel College.

Materials

Each couple/individual received a retirement planning workbook (Otto, 1980) and handouts produced by the workshop leader. Newsprint, markers, paper, pencils, and a chalk board were also used.

Procedure

The workshop was held on the campus of Thiel College, and was sponsored by the College's Center for Life Long Learning. The Center advertised the workshop through local newspapers and brochures, registered the participants, ordered or provided all necessary materials (excluding handouts), made arrangements for refreshments, and evaluated the workshop at the end. The registration fee was $45.00 per couple and $25.00 per individual.

The workshop consisted of six sessions, held from 7:30-9:30 on consecutive Wednesday evenings during February and March of 1984. A summary of the activities of each session is given in Table 1.

Session 1 ("Assessing Your Attitude Toward Retirement")—The objective of Session 1 was to enable participants to express and discuss their attitudes and concerns about retirement. Each participant introduced another person to the group, and explained why this person had decided to join the workshop. Next, participants completed "Facts and Fictions About Retirement," a handout consisting of 20 true-false questions about retirement (e.g., "Health and income are the most important concerns of retired persons"). "How Well Prepared Are You for Retirement?" was a 20-item checklist which posed questions one should be able to answer before retiring. For example, participants were asked "Do you know the cash value of your life insurance policies?" The first session ended with men's and women's groups listing their main concerns about retirement. The concerns of the groups were compared and solutions to the top three concerns of each group were discussed.

Session 2 ("Assessing Your Financial Situation and Budgeting")—The objective of Session 2 was to determine one's net worth and to develop a tentative, monthly retirement budget. Participants formed small groups to discuss problems they had encountered in determining net worth, a homework assignment from Session 1 (Otto, 1980, pp 22-3). Solutions were offered (e.g., asking the company pension officer what your retirement benefits might be), and

Table 1

A Summary of Workshop Activities

Session 1 - "Assessing Your Attitudes Toward Retirement"

　1. Another participants reasons for attending this workshop

　2. "Facts and Fictions About Retirement"

　3. "How Well Prepared Are You for Retirement"

　4. Men's and women's main concerns about retirement and some solutions

Session 2 - "Assessing Your Financial Situation and Budgeting"

　1. Problems in estimating one's net worth and some solutions

　2. Building a tenative, monthly retirement budget

　3. Resource speaker: Filmstrip and talk about Social Security and Medicare

Session 3 - "Assessing Your Housing Needs"

　1. Resource speaker: Lecture on common investments by trust officer of local bank

　2. My most important housing concerns

　3. Potential retirement sites you plan to visit soon

　4. Important factors to consider when selecting a retirement location

Session 4 - "Assessing Your Hobbies and Skills"

　1. "Show and Tell"

　2. Changes in use of time following retirement

　3. Potential activities and part-time jobs

Session 5 - "Assessing Your Health Needs"

　1. "The health habit I feel most positive about..."

　2. A health contract

　3. "Healthstyle: A Self-Test"

　4. Resource speaker: Lecture by dietician about basic food groups

Session 6 - "Legal Affairs and Conclusions"

1. What I have done during the last week to prepare for retirement

2. Location of important family advisors and documents

3. Measuring my progress in planning for retirement

4. "Unfinished Business"

5. Resource speaker: Lecture by lawyer on wills

6. An evaluation of the workshop

these problems and their solutions were then shared with the entire group. In the activity that followed, each couple/individual was asked to devise a tentative, monthly retirement budget based upon net worth, estimated future earnings, and knowledge of how retirement dollars are spent ("The Spending of a Retirement Dollar," 1981). Finally, a resource speaker showed a short film on Social Security and Medicare and answered questions.

Session 3 ("Assessing Your Housing Needs")—Because of time limitations in Session 2, the third session began with a resource speaker from the trust department of a local bank. He described investments that were frequently made by his 50 to 60 year old clients. The remainder of Session 3 was devoted to exploring desirable retirement locations. Each participant expressed his most important housing concerns, and solutions to the top four concerns of the group were offered. Then, each couple/individual compared the pros and cons of moving (Otto, 1980, p. 46), rank ordered the desirability of potential retirement sites, and set dates when these sites might be visited (Otto, 1980, p. 67). The session ended with a group discussion of important factors to consider before moving to a new community (e.g., cost, climate, activities, location of children, etc.).

Session 4 ("Assessing Your Hobbies and Skills")—The fourth session dealt with time management, as well as with skills, hobbies, and potential part-time jobs. For the "Show and Tell" exercise participants displayed an object which symbolized a favorite hobby. They were then asked to compare present use of time with anticipated use of time during retirement by dividing blank circles into pie-shaped sectors which represented activities now and in retirement. Afterwards, the whole group discussed how retirement would alter use of time. In the last exercise, couples/individuals listed potential retirement activities and part-time jobs, based upon an assessment of present skills and interests (Otto, 1980, pp. 80-86).

Session 5 ("Assessing Your Health Needs")—The objective for Session 5 was to emphasize the importance of holistic health habits. Each participant was asked to complete this sentence: "The health habit I feel most positive about is . . . " Then, each person was supposed to describe to the entire group a health contract he/she had made—an exercise that was not conducted due to time limitations. An evaluation of present health habits (e.g., cigarette smoking, alcohol and drug use, eating habits, exercise, stress control, and safety) was accomplished by completing "Healthstyle: A Self-Test." The session ended with a dietician's lecture on the four basic food groups.

Session 6 ("Legal Affairs and Conclusions")—The last session addressed legal affairs and pre-retirement planning activities yet to be completed. Each participant told the group what he/she had done during the past week to prepare for retirement. Couples/individuals then completed a form in which the location of important family advisors (e.g., Lawyer, accountant, etc.) and important family documents (e.g., deeds, stock certificates, will, etc.) were listed (Otto, 1980, pp. 102-6). The next workbook exercise consisted of a list of pre-retirement activities and participants checked those which were yet to be completed (Otto, 1980, pp. 120-2). Thus, each participant could measure the progress he/she had made toward planning for retirement during the workshop and also assess activities yet to be completed. Afterwards, each couple/individual provided the workshop leader with a list of three pre-retirement planning activities to be finished during the next six weeks and three to be completed during the next year. These lists were mailed back to the participants six months after the workshop (in September of 1984), as reminders of unfinished business. The last resource speaker, a lawyer, stressed the importance of having an up-to-date will. At the end of the workshop, a student employee of the Center for Life Long Learning asked participants to fill out an evaluation form.

RESULTS AND DISCUSSION

Attendance over the six sessions was fairly stable. Ten of the 14 participants (four couples and two unrelated individuals) attended at least four sessions; the remaining two couples, however, dropped out of the workshop after the first session. The reason for this early attrition is not known. Only three persons came to Session 4, due in part to hazardous driving conditions and in part to lack of interest in the topics covered.

The evaluation forms revealed a remarkable degree of consensus about what participants liked and disliked. The informal atmosphere of the workshop; the *Guidebook* (i.e., Otto, 1980); the resource speakers; and the workshop sessions on financial planning (Session 2), holistic health (Session 5), and legal affairs (Session 6) received the highest evaluations. In contrast, several participants suggested deleting the session on hobbies and skills (Session 4) from the workshop because they felt well prepared for retirement in these areas.

The author feels that the workshop served several functions which were not mentioned in the evaluation forms. It provided a vehicle for discussing concerns and expectations with peers, and emphasized that one retires to something rather than from something. More importantly, however, the workshop supplied a structure which stimulated participants to begin the pre-retirement planning process immediately rather than leaving the planning process to chance.

The author feels that his workshop compares favorably with similar workshops, such as SMART. Like many other workshops, this one emphasized small and large group discussions, the use of resource speakers, and the completion of homework assignments between sessions. In addition, spouses were encouraged to attend workshop sessions and to participate in all pre-retirement planning activities. In the author's opinion, the biggest advantage of his workshop over many similar ones was its independence from special interest groups. Many workshops are offered by insurance companies, banking institutions, or the participant's current employer. Under these conditions, many participants may feel they are expected to purchase something (e.g., an annuity policy) or they feel uneasy about speaking out on some issues that concern them about retirement (e.g., the company's pension plan). A second advantage of the author's workshop was its relatively short duration (six weekly sessions). Many individuals will be less hesitant to enroll in programs that make limited demands on time and will have a greater commitment to attend all sessions and to complete all the workshop activities.

This workshop demonstrated that the Lutheran campus may provide a suitable location for pre-retirement planning workshops, and that these workshops may be of benefit to college and community alike. Many of the physical resources needed for these workshops already exist on most campuses. Such resources as conference rooms, advertising capabilities, and secretarial help quickly come to mind. In addition, college faculties and staff can supply much of the human talent. Experts in such areas as dietetics, investments, real estate, health, recreation, and group dynamics can readily be utilized. Moreover, pre-retirement planning workshops can provide another vehicle for the Lutheran college to work with its alumni and with local parishes. Cooperative efforts in these directions could strengthen the bonds between the Lutheran college and its constituents. Alumni and members of local parishes could provide a new pool of participants or resource speakers for future workshops. Local churches might even prove to be convenient sites for these workshops. Finally, pre-retirement planning workshops can provide Lutheran colleges with a new source of non-traditional students.

CONCLUSION: FUTURE DIRECTIONS

The author plans to continue offering his workshop, but with several modifications. The workshop can be strengthened by modifying its content and by recruiting more participants. Based upon prior evaluations, Session 4 ("Assessing Your Hobbies and Skills") should be deleted, since most participants felt they had already developed the hobbies, skills, and interests that they will find useful during the retirement years. In its place, more specific information about financial planning should be provided through an additional resource speaker, such as an independent financial counselor.

The author is also taking active measures to increase enrollment for his workshop. Increasing advertising efforts may be one answer to the attendance problem. This might be achieved by providing inserts for church bulletins, posting brochures in information areas of local businesses, and directly contacting personnel officers of local industries. Taking the workshop off campus might also increase the pool of participants. The College could continue to sponsor the workshop, but the workshop might be held in the conference room of a local industry or the basement of a near-by church. These off-campus workshops could even be tailored to meet the needs of a more homogenous group, such as employees of a single industry.

REFERENCES

Darnley, F. Jr. Adjustment to Retirement: Integrity or Despair? *Family Coordinator*, 1975, 24(2), 217-26.

Healthstyle: A Self-Test. Public Health Service.

Hochschild, A.R. *The Unexpected Community.* Englewood Cliffs, NJ: Prentice-Hall, Inc., 1973.

McConnell, S.R. Retirement and Employment. In D.S. Woodruff and J.E. Birren (eds.). *Aging: Scientific Perspectives and Social Issues* (2nd ed.). Monterey, CA: Brooks/Cole, 1983.

Otto, E. *Retirement Rehearsal Guidebook* (updated fourth edition, revised). Appleton, WI: Retirement Research, 1980.

Rogers, D. *The Adult Years: An Introduction to Aging* (2nd ed.). Englewood Cliffs, NJ: Prentice-Hall, Inc. 1982.

Siegel, J.S. *Current Population Reports*, Series P-23, no. 78, 1979.

SMART (Senior Member and Retiree Training). Appleton, WI: Aid Association for Lutherans.

The Spending of a Retirement Dollar. Bureau of Labor Statistics, 1981.

Thurnher, M. Goals, Values, and Life Evaluation of the Pre-retirement Stage. *Journal of Gerontology*, 1974, 29, 85-96.